HOW TO FORM YOUR OWN MICHIGAN CORPORATION
BEFORE THE INC. DRIES!

A Step-by-Step Guide, With Forms

by Phillip G. Williams, Ph.D.

**Small Business Incorporation Series
Volume 3**

second, revised edition

The P. Gaines Co.

PO Box 2253, Oak Park, Illinois 60303

Telephone (708) 524-9033

Since laws are subject to differing interpretations, neither the publisher nor the author offers any guarantees concerning the information contained in this publication or the use to which it is put. Although this publication is designed to provide accurate and authoritative information concerning incorporation in the state of Michigan, it is sold with the understanding that neither the author nor the publisher is engaged in rendering legal or other professional advice. If legal or other expert assistance is required, the services of a competent professional should be sought. *Adapted from a Declaration of Principles jointly adopted by a Committee of the American Bar Association and a Committee of Publishers.*

Library of Congress Cataloging in Publication Data

Williams, Phil, 1946-
     How to form your own Michigan corporation before the inc. dries! /
by Phillip G. Williams. -- 2nd, rev. ed.
      p.   cm. -- (Small business incorporation series : v. 3)
     Includes index.
     ISBN 0-936284-06-4 (pbk. : alk. paper) : $24.95
     1. Incorporation--Michigan. 2. Corporation law--Michigan.
3. Corporations--Taxation--Law and legislation--Michigan.
I. Title. II. Series.
KFM4413.5.Z9W55   1993
346.774'06622--dc20
[347.74066622]   92-35346
                                  CIP

Manufactured in the United States of America

Table of Contents

Chapter 7. THE MICHIGAN NONPROFIT CORPORATION   77

Chapter 8. THE S CORPORATION   81

INTRODUCTION

If you are thinking of starting your own small business or have already done so, you may find yourself perplexed by the large number of laws governing your business activities. At one time, doing business in the United States was a much simpler affair. Most business activity consisted of small manufacturers and merchants offering their wares and services on a local or regional basis.

Today, the current trend is toward economic concentration in the hands of a small number of multinational corporations, who own everything from breakfast cereal firms to computer manufacturers.

We are also experiencing, on the other hand, a rediscovery of the individual entrepreneur, who has become a new kind of folk hero. Even large corporations at present are trying to tap into the strengths of entrepreneurial thinking. Some have designated individuals or even whole departments to work independently from the rest of the company in quest of more creative approaches to their business problems.

While some of the most astute large corporations are promoting entrepreneurial values as a part of their own structure, many entrepreneurs find themselves in need of following the opposite path. They stand to gain from learning the techniques of business that major corporations practice. Incorporation itself is one such practice that many small businesses are learning to profitably adapt to their own purposes.

We may wistfully recall the past and may even work for a reduction in our increasingly unwieldy business and tax regulations, but we cannot completely turn back the clock. With greater complexity and sophistication of techniques here to stay, many small businesses today wish to take advantage of the corporate form of operation. A number of individuals as well as businesses can benefit from organizing their own corporation. Persons in administrative and consulting positions can often profitably quit their present jobs, form their own corporate firms, and sell their services back to their employers, to the advantage of both parties. Salespeople, writers, artists, and designers will, in many cases, stand to gain from incorporating, as will many others planning to start or already running their own businesses, whether it be a catering service or a construction firm. Professionals such as engineers, dentists, and architects may profit from incorporating their practices as well. Some of the advantages of incorporation include limited liability, greater financial flexibility, a low corporate income tax rate for retained earnings, and a host of tax-free benefits, such as tax-free life insurance, a plan that pays medical, dental, and drug costs and health insurance coverage, a tax-deductible salary-continuation and disability plan, a tuition reimbursement plan, free legal services, and corporate stock dividends that are 70 percent tax free.

The present book, designed to clarify the important business area of incorporation, is written specifically for Michigan individuals and businesses, providing a thorough discussion of the advantages and disadvantages of incorporation, tax angles, employee benefits, and a blueprint for setting up your own Michigan corporation. In the back of this book we provide all the forms necessary to organize a Michigan corporation. Chapter 5 covers the procedure for forming a profit corporation, while Chapter 7 deals with the nonprofit corporation. If you wish to form a Michigan professional service corporation as a doctor, veterinarian, dentist, public accountant, psychologist, engineer, architect, or other licensed professional, you will find this type of corporation explained in Chapter 6.

If you prefer to do your own incorporation without a lawyer, you are entitled to do so, since you are not required by Michigan law to use an attorney to incorporate your business. Since the average attorney fee for an incorporation runs from $400 to $2,000, you will save money by incorporating yourself. On the other hand, if you already have a prospering business and little time to concern yourself with the details of incorporating, you can find a competent attorney skilled in this area through the local chapter of the American Bar Association. If you do prefer to use the services of a lawyer to handle your incorporation, the information provided herein will help you ask the right questions of your attorney and make the most informed decisions. If you decide to fill out and file your own incorporation papers, we recommend having a lawyer review them, since even simple incorporations may have "complications." You will still save money by following this procedure, since the charge for this service at an hourly rate (approximately $75 to $100) will be substantially less than the full incorporation fee.

If there are unusual aspects to your incorporation which are not treated in the following discussion, we also advise legal consultation prior to filing the Articles of Incorporation.

Chapter 1. THREE FORMS OF BUSINESS OWNERSHIP

Generally speaking, the federal and state governments of the United States and their agents such as the IRS recognize three legal forms of business ownership: the sole proprietorship, the partnership, and the corporation. While this book is primarily concerned with the last category, the corporation, it is important to examine the other two by way of comparison. Each has distinct advantages and disadvantages.

SOLE PROPRIETORSHIP

If you operate your own business and have not incorporated or entered into a partnership agreement, you are automatically classified as a sole proprietor. In other words, a sole proprietor is one person engaged in a business for profit. The chief advantage of this form of operation is its informality. You can start up or terminate your business whenever you feel like it. The state or federal government cannot prevent you from starting this type of business, so long as it is not illegal. The sole proprietor can also freely mix personal and business finances, lumping all the money into one bank account or handling it however he or she pleases. Of course, the sole proprietor, like all business owners, has to pay taxes, so he must apply for a state sales tax number, keep records, file state and federal tax returns and follow all other procedures required by law. But as the least regulated of the three forms of business ownership, the sole proprietorship does not require permission from the state for its formation, operation, and dissolution. Furthermore, the sole proprietor may transfer the inventory of his business to personal use. In the case of the corner grocery store, the owner may simply choose to eat what he does not sell. If the store owner wants to take a chicken from his meat case or a cantaloupe from his fruit stand, he is free to do so.[1] If an employee of a corporation followed the same procedure, however, he would be guilty of theft.

The major disadvantage of the sole proprietorship is that the owner is personally liable for all the debts of the business and for any injuries caused to or by its employees acting in a business capacity. If your warehouse clerk drops a 50-gallon drum on his own head or on the head of one of your customers, for example, then you are personally responsible for the damages.[2] Therefore, as sole proprietor, not just your business assets are "at risk." If you owe creditors more than your business is worth or if a legal suit against you awards the plaintiff an amount in excess of your business assets, your personal assets as well—your bank account, your car, your home, your Persian rugs—may all be legally attached, and your salary garnisheed if you have other employment as well.[3]

Your liability as a sole proprietor is limited only by the totality of all your possessions, personal as well as business.

Realistically speaking, many small businesses have no choice but to start existence as a sole proprietorship if the owner does not have sufficient time and resources to deal with the greater complexity entailed by the corporate form of operation. If the enterprise prospers, however, incorporation will become, in time, an increasingly attractive option. An excellent book on starting and running a sole proprietorship is Bernard Kamoroff's *Small Time Operator: How to Start Your Own Business, Keep Your Books, Pay Your Taxes, and Stay Out of Trouble!* This book also includes a thorough treatment of accounting practices for your business and contains enough actual ledger sheets and worksheets to last for a full year. (This publication can be ordered from The P. Gaines Co. Please write or phone for details.)

---

1   It should be noted, however, that even the sole proprietor is required, for tax purposes, to keep a record of inventory adopted for personal use. This information is needed in completing the 1040 Schedule C form.

2   Insurance is one means of protection, although it is often an expensive way to limit personal liability. It may also be virtually impossible for the small business person to obtain at affordable rates. While corporations as well as sole proprietors generally carry insurance, if they can get it, the corporate form itself is a valuable protection against unlimited liability (with the exception of professional service corporations—see Chapter 6).

3   Every state has laws which exempt certain personal possessions from attachment to satisfy debts, so a creditor cannot literally take the clothes off your back. Chapter 7 debtors faced with liquidation of their assets have exemptions of $3,5000 on their home, $1,000 on their household goods, including furniture, utensils, books, and appliances, $1,000 on tools and other implements used in carrying on a profession, trade, or business, and, under Michigan law, a specified number of cows, chickens, and other livestock!

PARTNERSHIP

A partnership is a business for profit which is owned by two or more individuals. Partnerships resemble sole proprietorships, with special allowances demanded by the fact of more than one owner. Thus, the same advantages which the sole proprietor enjoys apply to the partnership as well, the lack of formal requirements being the chief benefit. There exist no special procedures for establishing a partnership; a simple verbal agreement is sufficient, although a written agreement in the event of future disagreements among partners is highly advisable. Termination of the partnership is automatic upon the death, disability, or withdrawal of one of the partners (unless otherwise agreed). Another important advantage of the partnership is that it provides a framework for individuals to pool their resources, including money, skills, and ideas. In a partnership, the sum is often greater than the parts, since it permits persons acting together to achieve goals that none could attain individually.

The federal government's Uniform Partnership Act defines a partnership as "an association of two or more persons as co-owners of a business for profit." This act regulates the activities of partnerships in every state. It stipulates that the partners share equally in the profits and the losses, unless otherwise agreed. In a partnership, each partner owes the partnership a fiduciary duty to put the business interests of the partnership first. If partnership business is being siphoned off by one of the partners for his own use without the knowledge and consent of the other partners, that particular partner is guilty of defrauding the partnership and may be sued by the other principals.

As in the case of the sole proprietor, the partnership must follow all procedures, keep all records, and remit all forms and payments required by the state and federal taxing authorities. The partnership itself is not a taxable entity, however. The partnership annually reports its income to the IRS on an informational return (Form 1065), and the individual partners include their share of the profits on their personal 1040 tax returns. Thus a partnership determines its income and pays taxes in basically the same way as an individual sole proprietor.

Like the sole proprietor also, the chief disadvantage of the partnership is the personal liability of each partner for the debts of the partnership. All partners in a business are individually liable for all acts of the business. If your partner(s) is (are) unscrupulous or unwise, you stand to lose a great deal more than your initial investment. In summary, the risks of partnerships are extensive, since partners have unlimited liability for all actions or omissions of the partnership or its individual partners, employees, or others acting in its name and behalf. Another disadvantage: When the assets of the partners are disproportionate and you are the partner with much greater assets, you forfeit more in the event that partnership assets are inadequate to satisfy creditors' claims. In such an eventuality, your house may be attached and liquidated to pay business debts, whereas your under-capitalized partner may lose only her truck!

Another disadvantage of the partnership is that each individual partner's profits are taxed in the year of receipt, whereas the corporate structure offers greater financial flexibility, often allowing you to spread profits over a number of years and thus reduce the tax bite.

Finally, under the Uniform Partnership Act there exists a special type of partnership called the "limited partnership," which combines aspects of a partnership and a corporation. A limited partnership has two classes of partners, defined as general and limited partners. The general partners assume the operation of the business. In a regular partnership, discussed above, all the partners are general partners. A limited partner, on the other hand, can invest in a partnership without involvement in its management and without the risk of personal liability. Unlike the general partner who has unlimited personal liability, the liability of the limited partner does not exceed the amount of his initial investment. Unlike a regular partnership, a limited partnership agreement, according to state law, can only be established in writing. Many types of real estate investment groups, for instance, will have both general partners who organize the venture and limited partners who invest in it. Interestingly enough, a marriage is considered a general partnership unless there is a written agreement in advance that it is to be treated as a limited partnership!

The Partnership Book by Denis Clifford and Ralph Warner provides an excellent source of information about the nuts and bolts of setting up effective partnership agreements. It covers evaluation of partner assets, disputes, buy-outs, and the death of a partner. This publication can be ordered from The P. Gaines Co. Please write or phone for details.

CORPORATION

A corporation is a legal entity separate from its owner(s), manager(s), or operator(s). As a "legal person," it can conduct business, borrow and lend money, sue and be sued. Wanda Gold decides to incorporate her business and forms Wanda Gold Enterprises, Inc. Although Wanda is the sole owner and operator, her corporation in the eyes of the state has a distinct life of its own, separate from that of Wanda. It will be expected to pay taxes like a real person, it may enter into contracts, be named as a defendant or plaintiff in a lawsuit, acquire and hold property, and so on. Unlike the sole proprietorship and the partnership, a corporation cannot be formed until you receive written approval from the state. The life of a corporation, its "birth," begins with the issuance of the Articles of Incorporation by the state administrator and ends with its voluntary or involuntary dissolution (as in the case of bankruptcy). The Michigan corporation statutes define the rules and procedures governing the formation, continuance, and termination of Michigan corporations. Before we examine the mechanics of setting up your own corporation, however, let's take a closer look at the corporation as a form of business ownership.

Limited Liability

The majority of individuals forming Michigan corporations will enjoy the advantage of limiting personal liability by means of the corporate structure. Limiting liability, in fact, is traditionally one of the greatest incentives for incorporating a business. A corporate owner or director is not, in most cases, personally liable for the debts of the corporation. Therefore, if a lawsuit is brought against Wanda Gold Enterprises, Inc., only the assets of the corporation itself will be subject to collection, not the personal assets of Wanda herself (with certain important exceptions noted hereafter). This fact can be very comforting to someone just starting out in business. From the standpoint of limiting liability, the corporate route may be worth it in terms of peace of mind alone. Not only will the owner and other stockholders not be liable for the debts of the corporation, over and above their investment in the corporation in the form of shares of stock. Risk ventures can also be undertaken with the same assurances—only the investment of the corporation will be "at risk," not personal property.

In the event of a financial disaster, corporations, like individuals, can go bankrupt. If your corporation suddenly owes creditors half a million dollars and the assets of the company are only $20 thousand, then the business could file for bankruptcy. Once the $20 thousand in assets was distributed to creditors, the bankruptcy court would declare the corporation to be legally dissolved and the remainder of the company debt would in effect be wiped out. You would then be free to start another corporation tomorrow with a new name, if you so desired. This is not, of course, a recommendation that you form a corporation and amass huge debts and then cancel them out by filing for bankruptcy. Not only would such an intentional attempt to evade payment of bills be unethical, but most creditors would be unwilling to extend a large line of credit to you in the first place unless you were an established customer.

If it were apparent, moreover, that you intentionally formed a "thin" (undercapitalized) corporation in order to escape payment of debts, you would in all probability not escape personal liability. The courts in such cases in the past have tended to subject the shareholders of such corporations to personal liability. The point is that in the event of a major unforeseeable disaster—a lawsuit, large casualty loss, and so on—bankruptcy is a final "escape clause" for corporations which, unlike the sole proprietorship and the partnership, allows your personal assets to remain untouched.

The cases in which liability is *not* limited by the corporate structure generally fall into one of three categories: (1) taxes; (2) instances of gross negligence, fraud, mismanagement, or malpractice (especially in the case of professional service corporations); (3) personal assets pledged to secure a loan.

Regarding the matter of taxes, remember that the payment of taxes is the lifeblood of the state and federal governments. Strict laws and penalties safeguard this form of governmental livelihood. In this delicate area, even corporations are not exempt from sanctions, and, in some situations, an officer or employee of a corporation can be held personally liable for failure to withhold and pay taxes (if this is one of the defined duties of the employee's position, as treasurer, for instance).

Second, professional malfeasance may also trigger personal liability, as in the case of a director or officer who mismanages or takes advantage of the corporation.[4] This type of misconduct most often involves plundering the corporate assets through actual theft or other instances of draining the company's financial reserves. Not giving the corporation the "right of first refusal" also falls under this category. Other fraudulent acts, such as "doctoring" the corporate balance sheets, may result in personal liability as well. In such situations, the individual can be sued by the corporation and will be subject to personal financial liability for losses to the corporation. In addition to actual damages, punitive damages may also be assessed, and the party may be subject to criminal prosecution. Corporate directors of several large American banks have recently been convicted of this type of misconduct.

Under this same heading, it is important to realize that professional service corporations do not enjoy the same advantage of limited liability as other types of corporations.[5] A doctor or lawyer who has incorporated his practice, for example, will still be personally liable for any acts of professional misconduct, including malpractice, in his role as a practitioner of his profession. (The Michigan Professional Service Corporation Act does not remove the limited liability of the professional as a shareholder of the corporation, however.) This does not mean that incorporating does not offer other advantages to professionals. It sometimes does, so that individual professionals may find incorporating an advantage. See Chapter 6 for a detailed discussion of the Michigan Professional Service Corporation.

Third, creditors such as banks naturally wish to limit their risks as much as possible. An owner of a small corporation will often be asked to pledge personal assets as security for a loan. Obviously, the shield for personal assets which the corporate form provides in other situations will not work in this case.

In spite of these three important exceptions, the corporation does provide a limitation of liability not available to the sole proprietor or the partnership. In the event of legal damages you must pay, due to in-

---

4   We are not speaking here of honest errors of judgment but of gross negligence and downright intent to defraud.

5   Professions authorized by the Michigan Professional Service Corporation Act include certified or other public accountants, attorneys, chiropractors, dentists, optometrists, physicians and surgeons and other practitioners of limited branches of medicine and surgery, such as osteopaths, doctors of medicine, podiatrists, and chiropodists, architects, professional engineers, and land surveyors, as well as other professions which require licensing or other legal authorization in the state of Michigan.

jury or loss to consumers caused by goods or services you manufacture or sell, your corporation will serve as a reliable umbrella, in most cases protecting your personal assets from attachment and liquidation. This advantage alone may be worth the price of incorporation for most individuals.

The Corporation as a Tax Shelter

The corporation as a form of business ownership can save taxes in a number of ways not available to the sole proprietor or partnership, including corporate income tax rates lower than personal ones in cases in which the taxable income of the corporation is less than $150,000, corporate pension[6] and profit-sharing plans, corporate medical reimbursement plans, and other allowable business deductions. The following examples show how federal income tax savings may be realized and income generated by incorporating, through a combination of lower corporate tax rates, benefit plans, and the structuring of the sale of a going business to the new corporation. The current three-bracket graduated federal tax rate for corporations taxes the first $50,000 of income at 15 percent; income of $50,000 to $75,000 at a 25 percent rate; and income over $75,000 at a 34 percent rate. (An additional 5 percent tax, up to $11,750, is imposed on corporate taxable income over $100,000. Corporations with taxable income of at least $335,000 pay a flat rate of 34 percent.) A corporation would pay $7,500 in federal taxes on $50,000 in income, for example, while a single individual would pay $11,375.50 at present in federal taxes on the same dollar amount. If your corporation is very profitable, however, its tax bracket may be higher than your personal one. In that case, you can still enjoy many of the advantages of incorporation but have your business income taxed at personal rates by initially forming, or later switching to, an S corporation format.

Example 1

If Wanda Gold (a single individual) has $40,000 in taxable income, she would pay $8,562 in federal income tax, whereas Wanda Gold Enterprises, Inc. with the same taxable income would pay only $6,000 in federal taxes. Tax savings are only the tip of the iceberg, furthermore. Consider the following situation. If Wanda Gold Enterprises, Inc. pays Wanda a salary of $25,000 for her services to the corporation, she would personally owe $4,362 in federal income tax under current rates. If her corporation showed a profit of $40,000 a year, Wanda's salary, assuming it is "reasonable," would be deductible from this amount as a necessary business expense, thus reducing to $15,000 the income taxable to the corporation. If the corporation has a retirement plan, a profit-sharing plan, and a medical reimbursement plan,[7]

---

6   The 1982 tax act in effect eliminated the past favoritism of corporate retirement plans over Keogh plans for the self-employed sole proprietor, but the tax shelter advantages of all such plans remain immense.

7   An individual taxpayer can also deduct medical, dental, and prescription drug expenses, as well as medical insurance premiums, if he itemizes deductions, but only to the extent that such expenses, when lumped together, exceed 7.5 percent of adjusted gross income.

however, the contributions of the corporation to each of these plans would also reduce dollar-for-dollar the corporation's taxable income. Each of these plans would provide a form of tax-free income to Wanda (while some of it would be direct income, some would be deferred income). At the same time, the corporation could deduct the full amount of its contributions as ordinary expenses. If Wanda Gold Enterprises, Inc. pays out $9,000 during the year in medical reimbursements and pension and profit-sharing plan contributions for Wanda, for instance, it will show only $6,000 in taxable income ($900 in corporate federal tax will be owed, in other words). Taking into consideration Wanda's individual income tax of $4,362 paid on her salary and the corporate tax of $900, a total tax of $5,262 will be paid for the year. Remembering that Wanda would have to pay $8,562 in taxes if she were on a straight salary of $40,000, a federal tax savings of $3,300 would be realized in this particular instance because of the corporate structure. Remember also that Wanda will have received $9,000 from the corporation in non-taxable benefits for that particular year as well, over and above the tax savings realized. Wanda's company could contribute up to $600 to her favorite charity, moreover, and deduct it from income as a business expense!

Example 2

You decide to incorporate a going business whose worth has been appraised at $220,000. By carefully structuring the sale of your sole proprietorship to your corporation, you can provide yourself a substantial, almost totally tax-free income for a number of years. Here's how one such plan might work. Accept only a small portion of the total value of the business, say, $40,000, in stock from the newly formed corporation. For the remaining $180,000, take back a note from the corporation. (You are lending the corporation the additional $180,000 to buy the business, in other words.) If the term of the note is set for four years, you will receive principal and interest from the note over the next four years, with only the interest portion taxable (the rest is considered a nontaxable return of principal by the IRS). The major portion ($45,000 from return of principal each year) of the proceeds from the note will be tax-free.

The above examples illustrate some of the many tax-saving devices available to corporations. These strategies will be discussed further in Chapter 4, "Taxes and the Corporation as a Tax Shelter."

Perpetual Existence, Formality, and the Corporate Image

Unlike a sole proprietorship or partnership which ends with the death, disability, or withdrawal of the owner(s), a corporation may have a virtually unending life of its own. This aspect of the corporation is traditionally referred to as its "perpetual existence." Of course, a corporation can be voluntarily terminated if the owner(s) choose(s) to dissolve it because of financial or personal reasons. Also, a bankruptcy proceeding, as mentioned previously, may result in involuntary dissolution. These exceptions notwithstanding, the corporation is a more stable form of business than the sole proprietorship or partnership because its life is independent of a particular owner or management team.

Besides increased stability, the corporate form also requires greater formality of business operation. This is the positive side to the larger number of regulations which govern corporations, as compared to other types of businesses. Symbolic of this increased formality is the use of the corporate seal on business agreements, such as the application for a corporate bank account or loan.[8]

The stability and formality of the corporate form will help to lend credence to your business in the eyes of creditors, banks, employees, and the like. Just as good will is an intangible yet very important asset to your business, so too does the corporate image play a valuable role. If you are involved, for example, in consulting, freelance writing, editing, advertising, or other types of loosely structured businesses, the Inc. after your company name may very well give you a decided edge over your competitors. The fact that you have chosen to incorporate will lend an aura of professionalism to you that often pays off literally in terms of increased sales and profits. The bottom line is that incorporating may be a wise investment in the area of intangible business assets, in addition to any other benefits realized.

Capitalizing the Corporation; Charitable Contributions

Two other areas unique to corporations are the special means at their disposal for raising money and their ability to deduct charitable contributions.

A closely held corporation can, of course, issue and sell additional shares of stock at any time in order to raise more capital. If your closely held corporation proves very successful in the market place, then at some point you may also consider "going public." A public offering of stock can often provide hundreds of thousands or even millions of dollars in capital to growing corporations eager for expansion. If your stock is publicly traded, furthermore, you also have other avenues of financing open to you, through the issuance of corporate bonds (notes secured by company assets) and debentures (unsecured notes).

Corporations, unlike sole proprietors and partnerships, also have the right to deduct charitable contributions up to 10 percent of income each year (larger contributions can be carried over to future years and deducted from income). If you have a particular cause you want to support, then your corporation provides you an ideal tax-free means of doing so!

---

8   The seal is not legally required by Michigan law, but a place is designated for its impress on corporate business documents and on stock certificates. Although, technically speaking, its use is optional in the eyes of the state, you may be asked for it on formal business agreements, such as the application for a bank loan or even the application to open a corporate bank account. Seals can be ordered from many stationery stores. A corporate seal is also included with the Black Beauty Corporate Outfit available from The P. Gaines Co. (see the order form in the back of this book).

SUMMARY: MAJOR ADVANTAGES AND DISADVANTAGES OF INCORPORATING

Advantages

1. One of the greatest advantages of the corporate form is that the owner(s) of the corporation is (are) not personally liable for the debts of the corporation (taking into account the exceptions noted above— malpractice on the part of incorporated professionals; directorial fraud, malfeasance, or breach of fiduciary duty, loyalty, and care; unpaid taxes; and loans secured by personal assets).

2. The corporation as a tax shelter offers a number of tax-saving advantages not available to the sole proprietor or partnership, including lower tax brackets in certain situations (if taxable income of your C corporation is under $150,000[9] and you personally are in the 28 percent tax bracket), tax-free income in the form of medical reimbursements, pension and profit-sharing plans, "free" life, accident, and health insurance, tuition reimbursement plans paying up to $5,250 per employee for either work-related or non-work-related educational expenses, group legal services plans paying up to $70 per employee annually, and plans providing employees with dependent care assistance worth up to $5,000 per year tax-free.

3. The perpetual existence of the corporate entity gives it increased stability, enabling it to withstand changes in ownership or management.

4. Subject to certain limitations, a corporation may own shares in other corporations and receive dividends, 70 percent of which are tax free.

5. The stockholder(s)-owner(s) of a corporation can operate with all the benefits of a corporation but be taxed at personal income tax rates if this proves advantageous, as in the case of certain closely held family corporations (see Chapter 8, "The S Corporation").

6. The capital of the corporation can be increased with relative ease by issuing and selling to oneself or to other investors additional shares of stock. Corporations also have the option of making a public offering of stock and of raising capital through the

---

9   Although corporate income above $75,000 is taxed at the highest rate of 34%, the first $50,000 of that income is only taxed at 15%, and the next $25,000 at 25%. Therefore, corporate income must reach about $185,000 before it is taxed *above* the current highest personal bracket of 28%.

issuance of corporate bonds and debentures.

7. As an employee, you can receive loans from your corporation.

8. The corporate image itself can be a valuable intangible business asset in your dealings with clients, employees, and banks.

9. Individuals receiving Social Security payments can use incorporation to escape the limits on earned income. In 1992, those 62 to 64 years of age can earn only $7,440 without penalty; the Social Security Administration will take $1 for each $2 earned above this limit. For those between the ages of 65 and 69, each $3 of earned income above the limit of $10,200 reduces by $1 the individual's Social Security benefits. By paying yourself no more than the limit in earned income and retaining the balance in the corporation, you would be able to withdraw the remaining income at age 70 when the limits on earned income no longer apply.

10. Under current law, one can use an S corporation to incorporate a stock portfolio or other passive income.

Disadvantages

1. One small disadvantage of incorporation is the added expense you will pay in terms of fees, but these are extremely reasonable in Michigan (some of the lowest in the country): the one-time incorporation fee ($10), the organization franchise fee (a minimum of $50 for profit corporations, $10 for nonprofit ones), and an annual report filing fee of $15.

2. In order to use small claims courts in many states, corporations (unlike individuals, sole proprietors, and partnerships) must be represented by an attorney. This is a decided disadvantage for the incorporated small business person who uses or intends to use small claims court to collect unpaid bills and who wants to save money by doing his own collections. In Michigan, the law has been liberalized to allow a corporate officer to represent the corporation in court; attorneys are not allowed to appear in small claims court. This "disadvantage" turns out to be an advantage instead, because of the legislative recognition of the unique needs of the small, incorporated business person in Michigan.

3. Unless your net taxable business earnings are at least $25,000, there may not be substantial tax advantages to incorporating (although other advantages, such as limitation of personal liability, will still hold). As a general rule, the higher your income, the more tax savings you will realize and the

more fringe benefits you will be able to take advantage of as a corporation.

4. If you incorporate, you will pay more Social Security taxes than you would as a self-employed person (approximately 2 percent more, at present). On the plus side, these extra taxes are fully deductible by the corporation as a business expense, but not by the self-employed individual. (Starting in 1990, however, when the self-employment rate and the combined employer-employee corporate rate of Social Security tax will each be 15.3 percent, self-employers will be able to deduct half their self-employment tax as a business expense.) The current higher rate of Social Security tax paid by corporations will not result in any extra Social Security benefits when you retire. In the case of a wife working for the incorporated business, the couple's combined Social Security taxes may seem doubly burdensome. Since a low-income spouse will receive more, upon retirement, from the spousal benefits derived from her husband's account than she will from her own account, her Social Security benefits are, in a sense, wasted, although required by law. In other circumstances, she will stand to benefit, however. In the event of her death, her minor children can collect benefits on her account. She may also choose to retire and start collecting Social Security benefits while her husband continues working. If the marriage does not last at least 10 years, furthermore, she cannot draw on benefits from her husband's account, so she will need her own retirement plan. Since, according to one study, the average marriage today lasts only about 9 years, the additional Social Security tax paid by the corporation on behalf of a working spouse may turn out to be a blessing in disguise.

5. You will be required to pay an unemployment tax to the state and federal governments to cover yourself as an employee of the corporation.

6. The increased paperwork in maintaining the corporate records and in filing two tax returns (individual and corporate) will be another price of doing business as a corporation. For 1984 and later tax years, most small corporations will be able to file the new short-form federal corporation return (Form 1120-A), so this will simplify matters somewhat. The state of Michigan also requires the filing of a Single Business Tax return for any business activity, incorporated or not, with more than $100,000 in annual gross income (for tax year 1992). If you are knowledgeable about tax laws and normally file your own tax returns, you may well be able to continue doing so for your corporation. If not, you will need to hire a tax preparer or accountant to handle the filings.

7. If you are already operating a business as a sole proprietor or a member of a partnership, you may incur certain relatively minor expenses in notifying the public of your new status as a corporation, such as changing your telephone listings, having new stationery printed, and so on.

8. The fee charged by an attorney for an incorporation averages out to be around $1,000. Those willing to invest the time and energy to set up their own corporation, even if they have their incorporation papers reviewed by a lawyer, can still save most of these costs. Approximately one-third of all new corporations are formed without a lawyer, so if you decide to go it on your own, you are not alone!

TO INCORPORATE OR NOT . . .

We have given an overview of the corporation as a form of business ownership, in contrast to the sole proprietorship and the partnership, and have discussed some of the major advantages and disadvantages of incorporating. Subsequent chapters will deal in greater detail with the various topics introduced here. Before reaching a decision in your individual case on whether or not to incorporate, be sure to consider all the pros and cons. Plan to consult an attorney if there are special aspects to your situation.

CHAPTER 2. MICHIGAN CORPORATIONS

The first chapter was intended to acquaint you with the operation of corporations in general. In this chapter, we will focus on the Michigan corporation.

PURPOSES OF A CORPORATION

The Michigan Business Corporation Act defines the types of profit corporations that may be set up in the state and the laws governing their conduct. It is this Act that the following discussion will highlight. This particular Act does not apply to insurance, surety, savings and loan associations, fraternal benefit societies, railroad, bridge and tunnel companies, union depot companies, and banking corporations; these types of activities cannot be incorporated under this Act. Other types of corporations which will not be specifically considered in this book include cooperative corporations, secret societies, trustee corporations, corporations to provide student financial aid, educational corporations (including colleges and universities), educa-tional foundations, ecclesiastical corporations, and public building corporations (specific provisions regulating these types of corporations are covered by Michigan Act No. 327).

Two kinds of corporations excluded from incorporating under the Michigan Business Corporation Act but authorized to incorporate under other statues will be treated in this book in later chapters. These include the Professional Service Corporation (discussed in chapter 6) and the Nonprofit Corporation (discussed in chapter 7).

In Section 450.1251 of the Michigan Business Corporation Act, the broad range of purposes for Michigan corporations is defined as follows:

"A corporation may be formed under this act for any lawful purpose, except to engage in a business for which a corporation may be formed under any other statute of this state unless that statute permits formation under this act."

Any "lawful" activity may be incorporated in Michigan under the Business

Corporation Act, with the exceptions noted. In filling out the Articles of Incorporation (see Appendix A in the back of this book), you do not need to describe or even specify the type of business you are incorporating.[1] The purpose of the corporation may be simply stated as follows: "The transaction of any or all lawful business activities for which corporations may be organized under the Michigan Business Corporation Act." We will focus on the for-profit corporation in the remainder of this chapter.

POWERS OF PROFIT CORPORATIONS

Section 450.1261 of the Michigan Business Corporation Act spells out the particular activities Michigan corporations are authorized to engage in. In spite of the legalese of the language, we suggest you read this list carefully. This will give you an appreciation of the types of power your corporation will enjoy in the event you incorporate your business.

1. To have perpetual duration, unless a limited period of duration is stated in the corporation's Articles of Incorporation.

2. To sue and be sued in all courts and participate in actions and proceedings, judicial, administrative, arbitrative or otherwise, in the same manner as natural persons.

3. To have and alter at pleasure a corporate seal and use it by causing it or a facsimile to be affixed, impressed, or reproduced in any other manner.

4. To purchase, receive, take by grant, gift, devise, bequest or otherwise, lease as lessee, invest in, encumber, sell, exchange, transfer, or otherwise acquire, own, hold, improve, employ, use, and otherwise deal in and with, any real or personal property, or an interest therein, situated in or out of the state.

5. To sell, convey, exchange, mortgage, pledge, lease as lessor, transfer, create a security interest in, or otherwise dispose of all or any part of its property, or an interest therein, wherever situated.

6. To participate with others in any corporation, partnership, limited partnership, joint venture, or other association of any kind, or in any transaction, undertaking, or agreement which the participating corporation would have power to conduct by itself, whether or not the participation involves sharing or delegation of control with or to others.

7. To purchase, take, receive, subscribe for, or otherwise acquire, own, hold, vote, employ, sell, lend, lease, exchange, transfer, or otherwise dispose of, mortgage, pledge, use, and otherwise deal in and with, bonds and other obligations, shares, or other securities or interests issued by

---

1 By contrast, corporations organized for educational purposes, nonprofit corporations, and professional service corporations all require specific purpose clauses in the Articles of Incorporation.

others, whether engaged in similar or different business, governmental, or other activities, including banking corporations or trust companies. A corporation organized or transacting business in this state under this act may not guarantee or become surety upon a bond or other undertaking securing the deposit of public money.

8. To make contracts, give guarantees, and incur liabilities; to borrow money for its corporate purposes at such rates of interest as the corporation may determine, issue its notes, bonds, and other obligations, and secure any of its obligations by mortgage or pledge of any of its property or an interest therein, wherever situated.

9. To make donations for public welfare or for community fund, hospital, charitable, educational, scientific, civic, or similar purposes, and in time of war or other national emergency in aid thereof, without regard to specific corporate benefit.

10. To invest and reinvest its funds from time to time, to lend money, and to take and hold real and personal property as security for the payment of funds so invested or loaned.

11. To conduct business, carry on its operations, and have offices and exercise the powers granted by this act in any jurisdiction within or without the United States.

12. To elect or appoint officers, employees, and other agents of the corporation, define their duties, fix their compensation and the compensation of directors, and indemnify corporate directors, officers, employees, and agents.

13. To adopt, alter, or repeal corporate bylaws, including emergency bylaws, relating to the business of the corporation, the conduct of its affairs, its rights and powers and the rights and powers of its shareholders, directors, or officers.

14. To cease its corporate activities and dissolve.

15. To pay pensions, establish and carry out pension, profit sharing, share bonus, share purchase, share option, savings, thrift, and other retirement, incentive, and benefit plans, trusts, and provisions for any of its directors, officers, and employees.

16. To purchase, receive, take, otherwise acquire, own, hold, sell, lend, exchange, transfer, otherwise dispose of, pledge, use, and otherwise deal in and with its own shares, bonds, and other securities.

17. To have and exercise all powers necessary or convenient to effect any purpose for which the corporation is formed.

18. To participate as a member of any mutual insurance company for purposes of insuring property or activities relative to nuclear facilities owned, operated, constructed, or being constructed by the corporation.

THE EYES AND EARS OF THE CORPORATION

Since the corporation is a fictitious person, the actual work of the corporation must be carried on by real people. These individuals who conduct the business of the corporation fall into four basic categories,[2] according to their roles:

Incorporators
Directors
Officers
Shareholders

Many corporations will also have other employees or workers, in addition to the officers who run the business on a day-to-day basis. In a one-man or one-woman corporation, a single individual will play all these parts. Wanda Gold may wear all the hats at Wanda Gold Enterprises, Inc. In a larger corporation, these jobs will be divided among separate individuals. Even here there is generally some overlapping, however, particularly between the board of directors and officers of the corporation. At A.T.& T., for example, Robert Allen is both chairman of the board of directors and chief executive officer (president).

Incorporators

The incorporators, also referred to in common parlance as the "promoters" of the corporation, are the persons who sign the Articles of Incorporation and who make practical arrangements to set up the corporation.

Such arrangements may include a broad canopy of activities, from drawing up employment contracts and leasing office space to naming the initial board of directors. (It is advisable for legal reasons, however, to postpone making employment contracts, renting office space, and entering into other types of contractual agreements until after the corporation has been formed.)

Although we have referred to "incorporators," the minimum number of such individuals required by Michigan law is at present only one. Unlike some states, there is no minimum age limit for incorporators in Michigan.

The incorporator(s) is (are) responsible for raising start-up capital for the corporation. Some states specify a minimum amount of capital which a corporation must raise before commencing business. Michigan, like New York, California, and recently, Illinois, does not specify by law a minimum dollar amount as a prerequisite to incorporating.

From a practical standpoint, however, most any business will require working capital. From a legal standpoint, your

---

2   These categories exist in virtually *all* corporations, but we are concerned in the following discussion primarily with the specific delimitations of these categories in the Michigan statutes.

corporation should have at least enough capital to begin operations and to pay foreseeable, short-range expenses. If not, your "thin" (undercapitalized) corporation may run into legal problems, resulting in your being subjected to personal liability by the courts for the corporation's unpaid debts. If you already have an existing business, then as incorporator you can transfer assets from it in return for shares of stock.[3]

In the event that you are starting your Michigan corporation from scratch, you will need either to provide seed money from your personal funds (a portion of which may be in the form of loans to the corporation) or to find investors to capitalize the corporation in exchange for stock. Later in this chapter we will look at the role of the stockholder, whether that of the incorporator herself or other investors.

Directors

The board of directors (which may consist of a single director in Michigan) oversees the business operations of the corporation. The number of directors shall be fixed by, or in the manner provided in, the bylaws, unless the Articles of Incorporation fix the number. The Articles may also provide that there not be a board of directors and that one or more shareholders manage the corporation under a so-called "shareholders' agreement" (Section 450.1463). The duties of the board of directors ordinarily include making major policy decisions and managing the distribution of money. The board of directors typically decides when and how much the company will pay out in dividends to its stockholders and how much will remain in the company for its capital needs, research and development, ordinary business expenses, and so on.

Directors of Michigan corporations do not have to be of a set age or residents of this state. They shall have such qualifications, if any, as are stated in the Articles of Incorporation or the corporate bylaws. It is common practice for directors to serve without pay, since their work is ordinarily performed in order to increase the value of their stock holdings in the corporation. Directors in Michigan do not have to be stockholders, however, so financial compensation (including pension, disability, and death benefits) is permitted by law as long as it is given for real services. In addition, directorial salaries must be authorized in advance at a meeting of the board of directors, subject to approval of the shareholders if the Articles of Incorporation so provide.

Traditionally, the board of directors meets once a month, although the small corporation can often get by with one annual meeting (usually held on the same day as, and immediately after, the annual shareholders' meeting). Of course, special meetings may also be called at any time during the year in order to document a formal resolution, for instance, a directors' resolution authorizing

---

3 See Chapter 5 for specific recommendations regarding the transfer of assets from an existing business and start-up loans for your corporation.

a bank loan. Informal meetings or even phone conferences may also be held to decide a particular issue. In such cases, the directors should sign a written consent setting forth the action so taken and file these consents with the minutes of the directors' meetings. Special meetings shall be held upon notice as prescribed in the bylaws. A majority of directors is necessary to constitute a quorum for a meeting of directors, unless the Articles of Incorporation or corporate bylaws provide for a larger or smaller number. The vote of a majority of the directors present at the meeting constitutes the action of the board unless the vote of a larger number is required by the Articles of Incorporation or the corporate bylaws. Amendment of the bylaws by the board requires the vote of not less than a majority of the members of the board then in office unless the Articles of Incorporation or bylaws provide that the power to adopt new bylaws or amend bylaws is reserved exclusively to the shareholders.

Appendix D contains forms for the Minutes of the First Meeting of the Board of Directors. Recommended instructions for filling out these forms are included in Chapter 5. Even if you are the only director/officer of the corporation, you are required to keep minutes for the first and all subsequent director meetings and file them permanently with the corporate records (unless you choose to dispense with the board of directors and state in the Articles of Incorporation that the corporation will be managed under a "shareholder's agreement"). They contain vital information about your company regarding annual compensation, the issuance of stock, new

or amended corporate bylaws, the election of officers, and so on.

The directors are always elected by the stockholders. This election may be a mere formality when the corporation has only one or two stockholders who choose themselves as directors. In a large corporation, this is one of the main functions of the stockholders, to vote for the board of directors. The Michigan Business Corporation Act provides for a maximum term of three years for directors from the date of election until successors are elected. If the Articles of Incorporation or bylaws do not specify the terms of directors, however, an annual election of directors shall be held. Since the Michigan statutes do not forbid a director from running for re-election, you may continue to elect the same director(s) year after year. Further discussion of the voting procedures for the election of directors will follow in the section on "Shareholders" hereafter.

Unless otherwise provided by the Articles of Incorporation or bylaws, a director or the entire board may be removed, with or without cause, by vote of the holders of a majority of the shares entitled to vote at an election of directors. The Articles of Incorporation may require a larger vote for removal without cause.

A director may resign by written notice to the corporation. The resignation is effective upon its receipt by the corporation or a later time as set forth in the notice of resignation.

Directors may also propose a resolution dissolving the corporation in the event of bankruptcy, the expiration of the period of existence of a limited-life corporation specified in its Articles of Incorporation, or the cancellation of the Articles for failure to file annual reports or excise tax returns or pay taxes due, when the corporation has not been reinstated or does not desire to be reinstated. The resolution to dissolve the corporation must be approved by vote of the holders of a majority of the shares of the corporation.

Officers

The primary officers of a corporation ordinarily consist of a president, a secretary, and a treasurer, and, if desired, a chairman of the board and one or more vice-presidents. Other officers or assistants may also be elected, as needed, as specified in the bylaws. Unless otherwise provided in the Articles of Incorporation or bylaws, the officers shall be elected or appointed by the board of directors (some corporations, for instance, may give this right to the shareholders). None of the officers need be a director, but, in a closely held corporation, some, if not all, of the officers will undoubtedly be chosen from among the directors. The officers are in charge of running the corporation on a day-to-day basis. Therefore, a large corporation will require many more officers than a small corporation. The exact duties of the officers are either defined in the corporate bylaws or by the board of directors. To avoid confusion, the bylaws should state the officer titles of your corporation as well as their duties, which, of course, may be customized according to the particular needs of your business. Generic descriptions of the usual four—

president, vice-president, secretary, and treasurer—are included in the sample bylaws in Appendix B.

In Michigan, any two or more offices may be held by the same person. An officer elected or appointed shall hold office for the term for which he is elected or appointed and until his successor is elected or appointed and qualified, or until his resignation or removal. Unless otherwise provided in the Articles of Incorporation or bylaws, the officers shall be elected or appointed by the board of directors. The sample bylaws in Appendix B specify officer elections by the board of directors, at either an annual meeting or a special meeting. An officer elected or appointed by the board may be removed with or without cause. An officer elected by the shareholders may be removed, with or without cause, only by vote of the shareholders, but his authority to act as an officer may be suspended by the board for cause. An officer may also resign by written notice to the corporation.

Our friend Wanda as sole director-shareholder, for example, may hold all four offices of president, vice-president, secretary, and treasurer of Wanda Gold Enterprises, Inc., if the bylaws or Articles so allow. If her brother Junior is also willing to serve as an officer, they may decide to divide these four positions between them. Wanda, for instance, can be (1) president and vice-president (in theory, although in reality this combination would not be a good choice, since the vice-president normally "substitutes" for the president in his absence) or (2) president and treasurer or (3) vice-president and secretary or (4) secretary and treasurer or (5) vice-president and treasurer, or (6) president and secretary of the corporation, with Junior holding the other two offices remaining in each case. Or Wanda may choose to hold three offices and Junior one, or vice versa. If their mother Giesela is also an officer, then the three of them can divide up the four positions any way they choose. There is a wide range of flexibility in this area.

As in the case of directors, a sole stockholder-director does not have to hold all the offices unless he chooses to do so. He can find other persons to fill additional offices if he so desires, by enlisting other relatives, friends, business acquaintances as officers. Or you may wish to designate that your corporation will have only one executive office, that of president, which you yourself will fill.

As noted above, sample bylaws which define the duties of the main offices of president, vice-president, secretary, and treasurer are included in Appendix B, with the provision that the board may create other offices considered necessary. The president is the chief executive officer who directs the business affairs of the corporation. He or she has the power to "bind" the corporation in contracts and in debt obligations. Other duties, such as the power to hire and fire employees, vary from one corporation to another and should be spelled out in the bylaws. The vice-president assumes the duties of the president in case of his absence or disability and performs other duties as prescribed by the board of directors. Unlike the president, however, he or she does not normally have the power to bind the cor-

poration unless authorized to do so in a specific circumstance. The secretary keeps the minutes of all the meetings of the directors and shareholders and is in charge of the bylaws of the corporation and the share register showing the names and addresses of the shareholders. The secretary also notifies the shareholders and directors of meetings, has charge of the corporate seal, and assumes other duties specified by the president or the board of directors. The treasurer keeps the account books of the corporation, makes deposits of money, pays creditors, and prepares and presents financial reports on the corporation to the president and board of directors. The manner and nature of performance of the duties of the corporate officers are subject to the final authority of the directors.

The salaries of the officers are set by the board of directors, subject to approval of the shareholders if the Articles of Incorporation or bylaws so provide. As in the case of the salaries of directors, compensation must be reasonable and given for real services to the corporation. If your business chooses not to pay its stockholder-officers a salary but opts instead to repay their efforts on behalf of the corporation exclusively through stock dividends, the bylaws should so state.

Shareholders
Like the limited partners of a partnership agreement, the shareholders of a corporation are under no obligation to the creditors of the corporation or to the corporation itself, beyond paying the full amount due for shares they purchase. If Wanda Gold is the

sole shareholder of her company, as shareholder she has no legal obligation to the corporation after paying for her stock. It is in her additional role as director and officer that she owes the corporation a fiduciary duty. That is, she must look out for the best interests of the corporation, act honestly in her business dealings with it, give the corporation the right of first refusal, etc.

Besides providing capital and thus, quite literally, owning the corporation, the shareholders have several other functions as well. Most importantly, as already pointed out, they vote for the board of directors. Each outstanding share of the corporation is entitled to one vote, unless otherwise provided in the Articles of Incorporation, and, except as otherwise provided in the Articles, directors shall be elected by a plurality of votes cast at an election.

In Michigan, the Articles of Incorporation may provide for cumulative voting. Under cumulative voting procedures, each shareholder has the right to cumulate such voting power as he possesses and to give one directorial candidate as many votes as the number of directors to be elected multiplied by the number of his shares equals, or to divide his votes on the same principle between two or more candidates as he so desires. The purpose of cumulative voting is to protect the interest of minority stockholders. An example will show how it works. Take the case of Joe Stockholder, who owns 20 shares of stock in Wonder Widgets, Inc., a closely held Michigan corporation which presently has three positions on the board of directors to be filled.

If cumulative voting procedures are in effect, Joe will have 60 votes to cast in whatever manner he wishes. If Mary Public, the only other stockholder in the same corporation, owns 30 shares, her total voting power will amount to 90 votes. Even though Joe is a minority shareholder, by cumulating all of his 60 votes for one candidate, he has the ability to elect at least one representative to the board of directors, while Mary has sufficient votes to elect the other two. Without cumulative voting, however, Joe would receive *no* representation on the board of directors, since Mary would always be able to outvote him under normal voting procedures. Joe does not, by the way, have to pool all of his votes behind one candidate. He can use his votes in any combination that he desires, dividing them among two or even three candidates. Only by voting all of his shares for one candidate, however, can he be assured of electing his own man (or woman!) to the board. Cumulative voting, if it is, in fact, provided for in the Articles of Incorporation, can only be used for the election of directors to the board. Cumulative voting *cannot* be employed for other matters brought before the shareholders for a vote.

Shareholders also have certain other rights defined by the Michigan Business Corporation Act. Shareholders' approval by a majority is required for mergers and consolidations of the corporation with another in certain situations and for the amendment of the Articles of Incorporation. In addition, voluntary dissolution of the corporation may be elected by a majority vote of the shareholders. Just as the shareholders participate in the profits of the corporation through dividends, so too would they share in the distribution of the assets of the corporation upon voluntary or involuntary dissolution.

SALE OF STOCK

The Michigan Business Corporation Act specifies that corporate stock may be paid, in whole or in part, in money or in other property, tangible or intangible, or in labor or services performed or to be performed for the corporation for its benefit or in its organization or reorganization. This initial amount of payment for stock can be in cash or in other assets, including equipment (for example, a truck, restaurant fixtures, tables and chairs), inventories, accounts receivable, etc. Therefore, if you as sole owner of a business have capital assets consisting of any combination of cash and/or property, then you can exchange all, or a portion of, these assets for stock to begin business as a corporation. During the course of your operation as a corporation, you may take part of your compensation for actual work performed in the form of additional shares of stock. This is a common practice of many business executives of both small and large corporations, enabling them frequently to amass large stock portfolios.

On the Michigan Articles of Incorporation form, you will be asked to specify the type of stock to be issued, whether common or preferred. In the past, the form also asked the incorporator(s) to specify whether the shares had par value or not. All references to par value have now been eliminated, making the incorporation process simpler.

A few words of explanation will be given at this point about par value, since the records of the corporation and its stock certificates would ordinarily indicate whether the stock of the corporation has par value or not. The par value of a preferred stock represents the dollar value on which the stock's dividend is based. For instance, a 10% preferred, $20 par stock would pay an annual dividend of $2.00 per share (10% of $20). Most small corporations do not issue preferred stock, however.

In regard to common stock, par value is an arbitrary dollar amount which may be assigned to each share of a company's common stock under the company's charter issued by the state when it incorporates. It is primarily a bookkeeping device. Stock with a par value of, say, $10 cannot be sold when originally issued for less than its face value, whereas no par-value stock can be sold at any value set by the board of directors or stockholders. If the corporation goes bankrupt, the stock with a par value of $10 will not be worth $10 but will, in many cases, be worthless. The par value of a common stock has no relation to the market value or liquidation value of that stock.Therefore, its real value at any given moment, like that of no par-value stock, depends upon the financial condition of the corporation.

It is ordinarily simpler for most small corporations to issue common, no par-value stock, due to the greater leeway in allocating funds within the corporation from the sale of this type of stock.[4]

The Michigan Articles of Incorporation form also asks the incorporator to specify the number of shares of stock authorized. Theoretically, these numbers can be almost anything, for instance, from 1 to 100,000 shares of stock might be authorized and issued. In practice, however, we recommend the following guidelines: **(1) The number of authorized shares should be greater than the number actually issued. (2) The number of authorized shares should be the maximum allowable (60,000) for the minimum organization fee ($50).**

If you authorized 60,000 shares but issued only 1000 no par-value shares of the authorized number for a consideration of $10,000 of stated capital, you would later be able to make additional issues of shares without further report to the Department of Commerce.[5] In this way, you can increase the capital of your corporation in the future if need be by issuing and buying additional shares of stock yourself. Or you may decide to sell shares to other investors, reward an employee with a gift of stock, or transfer part of the ownership of the company to other family members through donations of stock.

The Michigan Business Corporation Act permits corporations to have different classes of stock, such as voting and non-voting. These rights and limitations must be spelled out in the Articles of Incorporation; otherwise, every share of stock is entitled to vote. In the past, you were not allowed under federal law to adopt Subchapter S status, discussed in Chapter 8, if your corporation had both voting and non-voting stock. The Subchapter S Revision Act of 1982 has eliminated this requirement, however, effective January 1, 1983. Some family corporations who want to keep control of the corporation within the hands of several family members while giving other family members (say, their children or retired parents) shares of stock may want to devise voting and non-voting classes of stock. Legal counsel is advisable in such a case.

---

4   In the case of par-value stock, if the face value is $10 and the stock sells for $12, $10 of every $12 received as payment must go into the capital reserves;the $2 excess constitutes capital surplus. In the case of no par-value stock, gains from its sale may be allocated between stated capital and capital surplus in any proportion decided by the board.

5   No further report (and filing) expense would be required as long as you did not issue more shares than the number authorized in the original Articles of Incorporation. It pays to plan ahead. If you do later wish to authorize additional shares, a certificate of amendment to the Articles must be filed along with a filing fee of $10 plus a minimum franchise fee of $30.

Chapter 3. SHOULD I FORM A DELAWARE CORPORATION?

There are a number of books on the market today which advocate forming a Delaware corporation, regardless of which state you live and do business in. These books are invariably written and published by Delaware companies who want to sell you their services as "registered agents."[1] Nevada, like Delaware, is another state that actively courts out-of-state businesses to incorporate in Nevada. There is nothing illegal about forming a Delaware or Nevada corporation, even if you are doing business exclusively in Michigan. Whether it is advisable is another question. An objective look at the issue of whether a Delaware corporation is recommended for the Michigan small business person follows.

In the past, certain businesses in Michigan and other states did find it advantageous to incorporate out of state because of tax and legal loopholes. All states, including Michigan, have now closed these loopholes. You cannot avoid Michigan taxes and fees by forming a Delaware corporation, as we shall see.

Those publications which recommend Delaware corporations sometimes imply that persons residing in other states with minimum capitalization requirements can bypass these requirements by means of a Delaware corporation, since Delaware has no minimum capital requirement for beginning a corporation. Michigan, like Delaware, does not fix by law a specific minimum capitalization for new corporations. Delaware corporations, therefore, do not hold an advantage over Michigan ones in this regard. In reality, no one ordinarily starts a corporation without any capital whatsoever. This is a very risky proposition, from both a financial and a legal standpoint. (See the discussion of "thin" corporations in the previous chapter.) Even in states that do have minimum capital requirements (generally a $500 or $1,000 minimum), this minimum is certainly a "bare" minimum. Almost all businesses would require more than this sum as start-up working capital.

One conceivable case in which you might choose to form an out-of-state corporation is if you are under 21 years of age and you

---

1   If you form a Delaware corporation but your business is located in another state, you would require a registered agent with a Delaware mailing address who would forward your Delaware Articles of Incorporation, annual reports, and other official papers from the state of Delaware to you.

reside in a state that has a specific age requirement for incorporators. Currently, some 30 states do have such an age requirement, while several others specify only that the incorporator must be "capable to contract." Michigan and 17 other states (including Delaware) have no statute governing the minimum age of incorporators. Therefore, it is a perfectly acceptable procedure for you to incorporate a business in Michigan and even be a sole stockholder, although you are legally a "minor." A Delaware corporation, consequently, offers no advantage over a Michigan one in this regard either[2].

In summary, we began by observing that in the past it was advantageous for some Michigan businesses to incorporate out of state. Most frequently, these out-of-state corporations were formed in Delaware, because of the simplicity of the corporate laws and low fees in that state. Due to changes in the laws governing foreign corporations, there are very few cases where a Delaware corporation would now benefit a Michigan business person. The only exceptions to this general rule are very large, publicly traded corporations, which operate interstate or internationally. These types of corporations may gain certain technical advantages in such areas as voting rights by incorporating in Delaware. Some companies initially incorporate or later re-incorporate in

Delaware because Delaware corporate regulations sometimes make it easier for a company to defend against unwanted takeovers, for example. This is obviously not a problem that small, privately held Michigan corporations have to worry about. For the Michigan business person with capitalization under $500,000, a Delaware corporation is *not* recommended.

The distinct disadvantage of a Delaware corporation is, of course, that it will cost you additional, unnecessary expense, if you are doing business in Michigan (not Delaware). If you form a Delaware corporation, you will have to register in Michigan as a foreign corporation, as already mentioned. As a foreign corporation, you will pay the same initial filing and franchise fees as a Michigan domestic corporation and the same amount of annual tax on income and assets. Don't forget, however, that in addition you will have to pay Delaware license or filing fees and franchise taxes as well. These are not just extra, one-time expenses. You will be paying these double franchise taxes annually. Unless you plan to open an office in Delaware, you will also have to hire a registered agent to provide you with a Delaware mailing address. In general, those who advocate Delaware corporations for anyone and everyone are putting a large number of individuals to additional ex-

---

2   Even if you reside in a state that requires you to be 18 years of age or older to legally act as an incorporator, such a requirement comprises no real obstacle to setting up your own corporation if you are a minor. Incorporators do not have to be stockholders. Consequently, you can have an adult file the incorporation papers for you (a lawyer, parent, or friend, for example). This is a perfectly acceptable procedure which would allow you to be sole stockholder of a corporation if you so choose, even if you are legally a "minor".

pense and paperwork, with no offsetting advantages.

Also, if you form a Delaware corporation and fail to register as a foreign corporation with the Michigan Department of Commerce, you may be denied the use of the court system of this state for the purpose of initiating civil actions and will be personally liable for business debts and lawsuits. If you later decide to pay the fees in order to use the courts (or are detected and made to pay), you will owe all past due filing fees and franchise taxes, plus penalties. In addition to any other liabilities imposed by law, a foreign corporation conducting affairs in the state without a certificate of authority will be penalized not less than $100 nor more than $1,000 for each calendar month, not more than 5 years prior thereto, in which it has conducted affairs in the state without a certificate of authority. This penalty shall not exceed $10,000 and shall be recovered with costs in an action prosecuted by the Attorney General.

In short, unless you are actually planning to conduct your business in another state, it is easier, cheaper, and smarter for you to incorporate in Michigan.

Chapter 4. TAXES AND THE CORPORATION AS A TAX SHELTER

The tax man cometh, not only for you and me personally but also for corporations. In this chapter, we will consider the various taxes paid by Michigan corporations as well as some of the main ways of minimizing taxes through the corporate form of business ownership. Clearly, the corporation is the most advantageous type of business when it comes to minimizing taxes. When you incorporate, your salary is tax-deductible, your medical coverage (including insurance premiums) is deductible, your disability insurance premium is deductible, most of your life insurance premium is deductible, and practically all other business-related expenses are deductible.

MICHIGAN STATE TAXES

Michigan Single Business Tax
In 1975, the state of Michigan adopted an innovative type of tax structure termed the "Single Business Tax." This new tax was intended to provide an incentive for new investment as well as create a more stable source of revenue and distribute the business tax over a broader base of businesses than previously. Seven taxes were repealed with the enactment of the Single Business Tax: Michigan corporation income tax, corporation franchise privilege fee, financial institutions income tax, savings and loan association privilege fee, domestic insurance companies privilege fee, property tax on inventories, and intangibles tax on business. The Single Business Tax is not an income tax, measured by income or profits; it is based on the economic size or "value-added" of a business activity for the tax year. All individuals conducting a business activity in Michigan whose gross receipts for tax year 1992 exceed $100 thousand must file an annual return.

The Single Business Tax is a modified value-added tax on the use of labor and capital in the business activity. The tax is calculated according to three major components; the amount of profits, compensation, and interest paid. This tax base is then reduced by the purchase of depreciable property during the tax year, as well as by various other deductions and credits. The tax rate since 1975 has remained at 2.35 percent of the adjusted tax base. The tax is computed the same way for all types of businesses, whether sole proprietors, partnerships, or corporations. Of the approximately 350,000 businesses in Michigan, about 190,00 are required to file Single Business Tax returns each year.

State Sales Tax

Both incorporated and unincorporated Michigan businesses are required to pay sales taxes to the state, collected on retail sales. It is actually the consumer, not the business, who pays these taxes, but you as a business owner-operator are responsible for collecting the taxes in an orderly fashion and remitting them to the state at regular intervals. The Michigan sales tax rate is currently 4 percent of the amount of the retail sale.

Individual State Income Tax

Any profits distributed to individual shareholders during the year as dividends must be reported on the state personal income tax returns of the recipients. These dividends are taxed at the rate of all personal income in Michigan, presently a rate of 4.6 percent (down from 5.1 percent previously). This tax rate is subject to certain tax credits, including a property tax credit, which gives the most tax relief to senior citizens, the disabled, blind persons, and disabled veterans or the surviving spouse of a veteran; a home heating credit; a farmland preservation credit; and a solar energy credit.

Since dividends are taxed at both the corporate and individual level, this results in the famous so-called "double taxation" of corporations. You will want to take this fact into consideration when deciding if and when and how much in dividends to pay the stockholder(s) of the corporation. For most small corporations, double taxation is not a worry, since dividends do not have to be paid at all, unless the corporation accumulates in excess of $250,000 in assets. Most small corporations will pay out almost all their earnings in salaries and fringe benefits, and will pay *no* dividends at all. Such a typical situation does not result in any double taxation.

It is usually preferable to take money out of your corporation in ways other than paying dividends, as long as you are not violating the law. More will be said about this issue later in this chapter. Under certain circumstances, you will be required to issue dividends. The IRS has set a ceiling on the amount of money that can accumulate in the company at lower corporate tax rates without being distributed as dividends. For professional service corporations, such as the health professions and engineering, the limit of accumulated earnings is currently $150,000. For other types of corporations, the limit is set at $250,000. Certain exceptions, such as the need for additional capital to expand your business or purchase another, are allowed. A hefty tax penalty is imposed on businesses that exceed their capital accumulations limit without any justification. The corporate minutes of meetings will normally lay the groundwork of plans for expansion, contingency funding, and similar rationales for accumulating capital in excess of the normal limits set by the IRS. The problem with many corporations will be simply in reaching these limits, not in exceeding them!

The legal power to declare dividends rests solely with the board of directors, subject to Michigan laws. In some cases defined by the Michigan statutes, a corporation is not permitted to pay dividends. Basically, dividends cannot be declared or paid at a time when the corporation is insolvent or when the payment of dividends would make the corporation insolvent or when the payment would be contrary to any restriction contained in the Articles of Incorporation. If your corporation will have to pay large dividends to its shareholders on a regular basis, you may consider electing Subchapter S corporate status (See Chapter 8, "The S Corporation").

FEDERAL TAXES

Corporate Income Tax

As pointed out previously, the federal corporate tax rate is a flat percentage of profits. The three-tiered system of rates is shown in the following table:

Taxable Income	Rate of Tax
First $50,000	15%
Next $25,000	25%
Over $75,000	34%

An additional 5 percent tax, up to $11,750, is imposed on corporate taxable income over $100,000 (corporations with taxable income of at least $335,000 pay a flat rate of 34 percent).

The regular corporate income tax return is Form 1120. All profit corporations, except those with Subchapter S status (who file Form 1120S) in the past have had to file this return annually by March 15, unless an automatic six-month extension is requested. A new, simplified corporate form has been available since 1985, Form 1120-A (a corporate "short" form, in other words). This two-page return can be filed by all corporations meeting the following requirements:

(1) Gross receipts, total income, and total assets are each less than $250,000

(2) Any dividend income comes from domestic corporations, qualifies for the 70 percent deduction, and is not from debt-financed securities

(3) It has no nonrefundable tax credits other than the general business credit and the credit for prior year minimum tax

(4) The corporation has no ownership in a foreign corporation nor do foreign owners hold 50 percent or more of its own stock

(5) It is not a member of a controlled group of corporations, a member of a group filing a consolidated return, or a personal holdng company

(6) It is not in dissolution or liquidation, nor is it filing its final tax return

(7) It is not a Subchapter S corporation or certain other corporations required to file specialized returns

(8) It is not subject to environmental tax under section 59A or to liability for interest (relating to certain installment sales)

Most small corporations will meet all of these tests, and will find their paperwork greatly reduced by using the short form.

Individual Federal Income Tax

Like the State of Michigan, the federal government also taxes corporate profits which are paid out to individual shareholders as dividends. These dividends will be shown on each shareholder's Form 1040 as income and will be taxed at the individual's personal income tax rate. To escape the double taxation referred to above, you may want to retain the balance of the profits in the corporation so long as you do not exceed the ceiling on accumulated earnings. There are many other ways of taking money out of the corporation tax-free, some of which will be discussed below. If your corporation is very profitable or is overcapitalized in the beginning, however, you may eventually have no choice but to distribute a substantial part of the profits as dividends and pay taxes owed. Otherwise, you will be subject to the IRS "accumulated earnings penalty" already referred to. Another alternative which avoids double taxation and is often advisable for small, closely held corporations that must pay large dividends regularly is the formation of a Subchapter S corporation (see Chapter 8).

TAX IMPLICATIONS OF EMPLOYEE COMPENSATION AND OTHER BENEFITS

Salaries

The corporation may deduct on its corporate income tax return as ordinary expenses all amounts paid to employees as salaries. Such salaries must be reasonable and paid for actual services rendered to the corporation. In this regard, putting family members on the payroll helps to keep income of your business within the family. If family members who draw a salary are not performing duties commensurate with their pay, however, you may have to answer to the IRS. The tax code permits deductions only for "reasonable compensation." This requirement prevents corporations from passing unreasonably large sums of tax-free money to its employee(s).[1] The IRS disallows inflated salaries to be deducted, treating the excess instead as disguised dividends. It will be up to you to prove that the amount of salary of each employee is "reasonable" in terms of duties, qualifications, and skills of the employee, the complexity of the work performed, the size and profitability of your business, the standard of living in your locality, and the salaries of similar employees in similar businesses.

---

1   The employee is taxed on the salary at his or her individual tax rate, of course, but the corporation can write off the entire amount of salaries as a tax deduction. Dividends paid out are likewise taxed to the individual at personal income tax rates, but *cannot* at present be deducted by the corporation as a business expense. In other words, since dividends come out of after-tax earnings, they prove much more costly to the corporation.

The IRS also considers the relation of the salary of the owner-employee to other key employees; the larger the salary of other key employees, the larger the salary that can be justified for an owner working full time for the business. In general, more sizeable salaries can also be justified for persons who perform multiple executive roles and for those who head highly profitable companies. For such an owner who is by and large responsible for the success of the business, a salary which is 50 percent of pretax profits is not unusual.

Somewhere down the road, if you have a very profitable corporation and plan to increase your and other key employees' salaries drastically, you will need to exercise prudence and care. Salaries should be set early in the year by the board of directors and should be tied directly to individual performance and productivity. You may well be able to justify paying yourself a salary of, say, $500,000 or even more a year, given your investment of time and money in the business, but be prepared to argue your case. The IRS often routinely challenges large salaries of one-owner and other closely held or family-run corporations, but its rulings are frequently reversed by the Tax Courts. Judges have ruled $1 million to be reasonable compensation in some cases, but $70 thousand too much in others.

In order to help build a case in justifying your salary—if it is very large—you should keep a log of all your business meetings and other professional activities. You might also want to maintain a clipping file of help-wanted advertisements for positions similar to yours which specify a salary. Growth Resources Inc., a Peabody, Mass. company which publishes an annual executive compensation report based on a poll of small and medium-sized companies, is another good source of comparative salary data.

Geneva Cos., a financial-services concern in Irvine, California, has studied 2,500 closely held corporations' compensation by industry group. This data reveals a current median compensation for small business owners of $151,000 in businesses with annual revenue between $1 million and $100,000 million. Most highly paid were the owners of primary metal industries ($264,000 a year), while owners of garden and building materials supplies ranked last, with an average compensation of $108,000. "Compensation" in this survey included salary *and* benefits; salary itself amounted to approximately 78 percent of compensation.

Another possible move is to approve a resolution at a directors' meeting and record it in the minutes covering the contingency of an IRS challenge. The resolution would state that in the event the IRS rules officer salaries to be excessive, the officers in question can pay back the excess amount to the corporation; further, that the amount returned will be treated as a loan to the employees, for tax purposes. When you are paying yourself such a sizeable salary as to need to consider such techniques, then expert legal counsel would, of course, be advisable. It is also permissible to take a larger salary in more profitable years to make up for a smaller salary in poorer years, but, again, the corporate minutes should state that the salary for a particular year in question is above or below average, due to the financial state of the business. In general, you should avoid paying large lump-sum bonuses at the end of the year to yourself or other employees. Such bonuses look suspiciously like dividends to the IRS and may be treated as such for tax purposes, since they are paid after the company's earnings for the year are already known. In all tax matters, remember that the success of your claims before the IRS will depend primarily upon the degree of formality you have exercised in your business dealings and the reasonableness of your actions.

Tax-free Pension and Profit-sharing Plans

There are two basic types of pension plans available for businesses, (1) defined contribution plans and (2) defined benefit plans.[2] The former is much simpler to administer, because it limits the amount of actual contributions to a set dollar amount or a percentage of earnings. Under the 1982 Tax Act, a corporation can in post-1982 years make tax-free payments to a defined contribution fund up to the lesser of (a) 25 percent of each employee's annual compensation or (b) $30,000.[3] The amount of money available to the employee during retirement under this arrangement will depend entirely upon the return on pension fund investments.

The second type of pension plan, the defined benefit plan, is more complicated to administer because it pays the retiree a specified amount during retirement. The actual dollar amount of contributions permitted each year can only be determined by an actuary. The 1982 Tax Act permits corporations in post-1982 years to set aside sufficient funds in a defined benefit plan to fund a straight life annuity to the employee on retirement equal to the lesser of (a) $108,963 payout per year[4] or (b) 100 percent of the participant's average compensation for his highest three years. If you choose a defined benefit plan through an insurance company or a bank, it should do all the actuary work and present you with an IRS-approved master plan which you can adopt for your company.

Both types of plans provide tax-deferred benefits to the employee(s), since the funds are allowed to accumulate tax-free until withdrawn, at which time the employee is likely to be in a lower tax bracket. Since these contributions are completely deductible by the corporation as a business expense, they thereby lower the taxable income of the corporation as well. If the corporation is dissolved, the pension funds can be rolled over tax-free into IRA accounts for its employees.

One very important aspect of corporate pension plan set-asides is that such plans

---

2   Legal changes have placed retirement plans for unincorporated businesses more on a par with those available to corporations.

3   Down from the maximum allowable contribution per employee of $45,475 in 1982.

4   Down from $136,425 in 1982.

cannot discriminate in the owner-employee's favor. If yours is a one-owner corporation, there appears to be no question of discrimination. There are certain precautions that must be taken in such a case of the one employee who is a stockholder. In addition to being a bona fide plan and meeting the usual requirements, the plan also must provide for coverage of additional employees if and when they are hired. If your company has other employees, you will normally be required to cover them in your benefit plan as well as yourself. You may very well desire to include other employees in your retirement plan as part of your over-all employee compensation package. There are also certain cases in which employees can be excluded from coverage if you so wish. If your corporation hires "independent contractors," then not only will you not have to cover them in your pension or profit-sharing plans (since they are not considered employees), but you will also not have to withhold taxes from their salary or pay their Social Security deductions. Part-time employees (who work less than 1,000 hours a year) and those under the age of 21 can also be excluded from coverage. If you do wish to set up a corporate pension fund, particularly of the defined benefit type, you may need to see a tax consultant in order to insure favorable tax treatment and legality of this and other corporate "perks" for employees.

Another angle that you should be aware of is the fact that you can, in certain circumstances, act as trustee of your own corporate pension plan, enabling you to lend money from the benefit fund to yourself. As long as your company approves, further-more, any of the participants in its pension or other deferred compensation plans can borrow a portion of their contributions back. The 1982 Tax Act has set limits on these loans, however, because of past abuses in which certain individuals were borrowing the full amount of their tax-deductible retirement contributions. Under the new provisions of the law, the maximum amount you can borrow is $50,000 or half your vested money in the plan, whichever is less. You are allowed to borrow up to $10,000, however, even if that is more than half the amount you have vested. A further stipulation is that a loan must be repaid within 5 years, unless it is used to buy, build, or refurbish your principal residence. Terms for such home loans range from ten to 25 years.

SEPs

Another pension option especially attractive for the small business owner merits a separate discussion of its own. Simplified Employee Pensions (SEPs for short) offer a relatively new, hassle-free form of retirement plan available for corporations as well as partnerships and the self-employed. Unlike other types of corporate pension plans, SEPs entail no administrative expense and no burdensome paper work. For businesses with very limited resources, SEPs are ideal retirement vehicles because of the ease of setting them up and the benefits they provide, which compare favorably with other types of defined contribution corporate pension plans. They have a $30,000 annual limit or 15 percent of compensation, whichever is less. They offer flexible funding, furthermore, since they can be financed solely by the employer, solely by the employee(s), or a combination of the two. They also offer the advantage of being integratable with Social Security. Most importantly, you do not have to contribute to the plan in those years you choose not to do so, whether for financial or other reasons.

The P. Gaines Co. publishes a book about SEPs entitled *Five Easy Steps to Setting Up an IRS-Approved Retirement Plan for Your Small Business, With Forms.* This publication explains why almost any business that is profitable enough to pay its employee(s) a salary can establish an SEP immediately. It walks the reader through the procedure for setting up an SEP and includes all needed forms in appendices. See the order form in the back of this book for additional information about this pension plan guide.

Section 89 and Employee Benefit Plans

The Tax Reform Act of 1986 set up new, stricter rules for employee benefit plans. These so-called "Section 89" rules (the section of the tax code in which they appear) have been hotly debated. Some overly complex and burdensome parts of Section 89, largely affecting larger corporations, will, in all likelihood, be amended or repealed. The parts that pertain to small businesses, whether corporations, sole proprietors, or partnerships, are detailed below. Medical reimbursement plans, health and life insurance plans, disability insurance plans, and most other kinds of employee benefit plans are subject to these qualifications:

- A plan must be in writing
- Employees must be informed of their benefits, for instance, through a flyer detailing essential features
- Employees' rights under the plan must be legally enforceable
- The plan must be operated for the exclusive benefit of employees
- The plan must be permanent (set up with the intent of operating indefinitely)

Employees should receive notice of the basic features of your benefit plan(s) by July 1, 1989. All plans must be put in writing by the end of 1989. If at least 80 percent of a company's nonhighly compensated employees are covered by your benefit plan and the plan does not contain provisions which discriminate in favor of highly compensated employees, the plan qualifies for tax-free status. If the business has *only* highly compensated employees, your plan automatically qualifies. Most small businesses will meet these basic tests.

Note: At time of printing of this publication, the law mandating Section 89 requirements had been repealed. For the present, therefore, these rules do not have to be enforced.

Medical Reimbursement Plans

Corporate employees, their spouses, and dependents can also be covered with a medical reimbursement plan which pays the cost of medical expenses and drugs. All such corporate medical reimbursements are tax-deductible by the corporation as an ordinary business expense and are passed tax-free to the individuals receiving them.[5] Although referred to as "reimbursement plans" by the IRS, your corporation can pay your medical bills and that of your family directly instead of reimbursing you afterward. In a small or one-owner corporation, there is no reason why your corporation should not pay 100 percent of your and your family's medical expenses not covered by other insurance, provided there are sufficient funds to do so. Again, be sure to consult a tax adviser who specializes in this area to assure favorable tax treatment of the plan. In a larger corporation, it may be necessary to set a ceiling on the actual dollar amount paid out per employee each year.

A model medical reimbursement plan which you may adopt for use by your corporation is included in Appendix E. *This model plan provides for the payment of all medical bills, including premiums for accident and health insurance.*[6]

This coverage, like that of medical and dental expenses and drugs, may be extended to the spouses and dependents as well as the employees themselves. Accident and health insurance coverage does not have to be part of a "group plan" such as those offered by Blue Cross. You can choose your own individual plan and have the corporation pay for it.

Life Insurance

Other employee benefits which are tax-free to the individual and tax-deductible to the corporation include life and disability insurance and workers' compensation insurance. "Free" life insurance purchased by the corporation for its employees is limited to one-year renewable term policies of up to $50,000 coverage per employee. Such insurance plans are normally set up for groups of employees, although even a sole owner-employee of a corporation can qualify under IRS guidelines. The face value of the policy can exceed $50,000, but in such cases the IRS requires the individual to pay taxes on the "imputed income" above $50,000. Nor can the company take a tax deduction for the "excess" amount over $50,000. This taxable income is computed according to the age of the employee and the approximate amount of premium paid per $1,000. The following table from IRS

---

5   Whereas the corporation can deduct the total amount spent for medical and dental expenses for its employees, the individual taxpayer, as noted in Chapter 1, can deduct only that portion of expenses exceeding 7.5 percent of adjusted gross income.

6   Unincorporated business owners, whether sole proprietors or partnerships, are now allowed to deduct 25 percent of health insurance premiums paid for themselves and their spouses, subject to certain limitations. If there are other employees of the business besides the owner(s) they, too, must be provided coverage. If an individual owner is eligible to participate in an employer-sponsored plan, his business cannot also have a plan eligible for the 25 percent deduction.

Publication 525 summarizes these variables:

Cost per $1,000 of Protection for One Month

Age	Cost
Under 30	8 cents
30 through 34	9 cents
35 through 39	11 cents
40 through 44	17 cents
45 through 49	29 cents
50 through 54	48 cents
55 through 59	75 cents
60 through 64	$1.17
65 through 69	$2.10
70 and older	$3.76

You figure the cost for each month of coverage by multiplying the number of thousands of dollars of insurance, figured to the nearest tenth, by the cost from the above table. You must prorate the cost from the table if less than a full month of coverage is involved.

For example, you are 54 years old and your employer provides term life insurance coverage for you in the amount of $80,000. Since $50,000 is excludable from your income, you must figure the amount to include in your income of the remaining $30,000 in coverage. The cost per $1,000 of someone 54 years old is 48 cents (from table). Multiply this figure times 30 (the number of thousands of dollars of the excess amount). This figure of $14.40 (48 cents x 30) is the cost of excess insurance for one month. The amount for the year, $172.80 (12 x $14.40) is the figure which you would show on your personal income tax return as income.

You can also set up an insurance program that gives retired employees (including yourself) up to $50,000 per person of tax-deductible insurance. The retiree would be liable for taxes on insurance above $50,000. Furthermore, you can arrange for group life insurance for immediate family members of the corporation's employees.

Disability Insurance

Premiums paid by your corporation for disability insurance coverage are also deductible by the corporation and tax-free to the employee(s). Although the amount of disability insurance an employee can purchase is limited to a percentage of income, usually in the range of 33 to 70 percent,[7] for higher paid executives the premiums per year may amount to several thousand dollars in tax-free "income." Benefits paid under company-financed plans for temporary disability (illness or injury) are included in the employee's gross income and are subject to tax.[8] In the case of permanent and total disability, a partial tax exclusion of benefits is allowed. If the premiums for

---

7   Insurance companies limit benefits to avoid creating a disincentive to return to work.

8   The "sick pay exclusion" which in the past treated such benefits as tax-free income was repealed by the Tax Reform Act of 1976.

disability insurance are paid by the employee, however, all benefits, whether for temporary or permanent disability, are non-taxable.

Workers' Compensation

Workers' compensation is another form of insurance which is deductible by your corporation. Workers' compensation insurance set by state law covers any claims for bodily injuries or job-related diseases suffered by employees in your business, regardless of fault. This form of insurance is not even available to sole proprietors, but you are entitled to it as the employee of your corporation.[9]

Interest-free and Low-interest Loans

Another benefit which key employees or sole owner-operators of corporations have enjoyed for decades is the interest-free loan.

For interest-free or below market interest loans made or outstanding after June 6, 1984, the following rules apply. Such loans from the employer to the employee or independent contractor will be treated as though the employee or independent contractor received compensation equal to the market rate of interest that would have been due if the money had been borrowed from a conventional source such as a bank. This "imputed" compensation must be included in the gross income of the borrower; if the bor-

rower itemizes deductions, he can take an offsetting deduction for the imputed interest expense, however. In order to get the interest deduction at present, the loan must be secured by your home. The interest will then be deductible as home equity loan interest, unless you already have the maximum $100,000 of home equity debt.

Such treatment would normally produce a "wash," without taxable income to the employee, unless the loan was used to carry tax-exempt securities (in which case, no interest deduction is permitted). This interest-free loan "perk" can be made available to executives of a corporation on a discriminatory basis, that is, it does not have to be offered to all employees or even ones of a particular class or group. Such loans can be made for virtually any purpose from buying a home to financing a child's education.

It is important to note that loans under $10,000 are not treated as though an "imputed" amount of interest were received and then paid back. In other words, a $10,000 de minimis exception allows loans of this size or smaller to be treated in the old conventional way as interest-free and tax-free. The de minimis exception does not apply to loans structured merely for the purpose of tax avoidance, however.

Corporation-shareholder loans also are subject to the $10,000 de minimis exception. For loans in excess of $10,000 in this

---

9 A partnership, moreover, cannot deduct premiums paid for workers' compensation on behalf of partners, since partners are not considered employees of the partnership.

area, the imputed interest is treated as transferred from the corporation to the shareholder. Thus, the corporation is considered to have paid a dividend includable in the shareholder's income. The shareholder gets an offsetting deduction, however, and the corporation treats as interest income the amount of imputed interest.

The current rate of imputed interest will be set semi-annually by the Treasury Department, based on market conditions. The law does not make clear whether those individuals who have dual roles as shareholders and employees in a corporation are to be treated under the employer-employee rule or the corporation-shareholder rule.

If you have a corporate pension plan, you can also borrow from it, but the rules prohibit no-interest, below market loans.

Section 450.1548 of the Michigan Business Corporation Act authorizes your corporation to make loans to you as an employee, officer, or director when, in the judgment of the board, the loan may reasonably be expected to benefit the corporation. The loan may be with or without interest, and may be secured or unsecured, as the board deems appropriate. Such loans offer one attractive way of taking money out of your business for legitimate personal uses. It is important, of course, to exercise the proper formality in recording all such loans, by signing a promissory note and carrying the loan on the corporate record books under "Accounts Receivable." By following a fixed repayment schedule, you will avoid potential trouble with the IRS on the issue of whether the loan is actually a disguised dividend.

Tax-free Dividends

Dividends paid to you by your corporation are fully taxable as ordinary income. By contrast, if the same stock investments were made by your corporation, 70 percent of the total dividends would escape taxes. The limitations on what qualifies for tax-free treatment are spelled out in IRS Publication 542. Basically, all dividends from domestic U.S. stocks qualify for the 70 percent exclusion, except for dividends from a real estate investment trust and dividends from stock held by your corporation for 45 days or less (90 days or less for preferred dividends).

There exist mutual funds for corporations which invest in stocks that pay dividend income qualifying for the 70 percent corporate exclusion from tax. Two such funds are Vanguard Qualified Dividend Portfolio I (minimum investment of $3,000) and Fidelity Qualified Dividend Fund (minimum investment of $50,000).

Naturally, you will want to maximize your passive income earnings through dividends and other sources. One word of caution, however: you do not want to be considered a "personal holding corporation" by the IRS. A personal holding corporation is defined as a company in which 60 percent or more of corporate profits consists of passive income from stocks, bonds, rents, royalties, etc., and less than 40 percent of profits is derived from business operations.

If you do not limit your investment income and are deemed a personal holding company, you will be subject to especially heavy punitive taxes.

OTHER TAX-DEDUCTIBLE BENEFITS AND EXPENSES

The payment of rent, utility, and phone bills for business usage all provide legitimate tax deductions for your corporation. If your office is at home, then you will need to allocate your expenses between business and personal use. If you rent an apartment, it is a good idea to write two checks each month, one business and one personal, for the proportionate part of the total rent in each case. A proportionate percentage of other expenses such as water and electricity can also be deducted by your corporation.[10] If you have a separate business phone, then the total bill will, of course, be a business expense. If one phone serves both business and personal use, you should keep a log of all long-distance business calls and be sure to pay the full amount of these as a corporate expense. Before 1989, you could deduct the part of the base rate of your residential telephone allocable to business usage. Currently, the base rate of the first telephone into your residence is considered a nondeductible personal living expense, with no business portion allowable.

If you own your home and have an office therein, you can rent office space to the corporation. Rent paid to a stockholder is another area the IRS looks at closely, since excessive rent provides one way for owners of a corporation to take disguised dividends out of the company. Therefore, the amount of rent you charge the corporation should be reasonable in terms of the cost of comparable office space in your vicinity. If you use 10 percent of your home as an office, do not figure the corporate rent as 10 percent of your mortgage and taxes, however. Generally, you will be entitled to a larger deduction than this when you consider what similar office space rents for. You should draw up a formal lease agreement with the corporation, in the event of a future tax audit. You can also deduct "repairs" to the business portion of your property in the year incurred, while "improvements" must be amortized (deducted over the period of time they are expected to last).

Other tax-free employee benefits that may be provided include free parking, group legal services plans that offer up to $70 in legal services per employee annually (any amount over that would be taxable to the employee), subsidized lunches, and on-site physical fitness facilities. In the case of free parking, the employer can pay its employee parking expenses (this tax-free subsidy is currently unrestricted in amount). The employer may also provide up to $21 a month per employee as a tax-free mass tran-

---

10   A higher percentage may be justified for the business portion in individual cases. Your business may require unusually large expenditures for electricity and water if you are a professional photographer or a beautician, for example.

sit subsidy. The reimbursement of expenses for operating and maintaining automobiles and other motor vehicles used in your business are deductible either on a per-mile or actual cost basis. The depreciation of business equipment such as cars and computers is another form of tax-free benefit. An especially attractive tax break is the current law allowing up to $10,000 of business property to be written off in the first year that it is placed in service (instead of depreciated). Special rules concerning this write-off apply to cars.

Your corporation can also pay and deduct up to $5,000 as a tax-free death benefit to the beneficiary of any employee, including yourself.

Educational expenses up to $5,250 per employee are also deductible by the corporation and tax-free to the recipient. Your company could pay for tuition, books, supplies, and other education-related equipment for either work-related or non-job-related courses taken by employees (but not for those graduate courses leading to a degree in law, business, medicine, or other advanced or professional degrees). The eligibility of such a program depended on (1) its being in written form, (2) the giving of reasonable notice of the plan and its terms and availability to all eligible employees, and (3) its not being discriminatory in favor of certain officers, shareholders, or key employees, or spouses or dependents of such individuals. There was also a stringent restriction on the amount of benefits available to shareholders of the corporation: No more than 5 percent of the benefits paid or in-

curred by the employer during the year could go to that group of individuals (and their dependents) each of whom held more than a 5 percent stock interest in the company.

Other tax-free benefits include the cost of convention travel as well as food, lodging, and related expenses incurred by employees attending meetings to increase business know-how and to upgrade skills. Foreign conventions, with several exceptions, are generally not deductible, although travel abroad for business purposes is deductible.

Your corporation can also give you and other employees a discount on goods and services. The Tax Reform Act of 1984 placed a limit on the amount of such tax-free discounts. The discount is now limited to your "gross profit percentage." If your profit margin averages 30 percent, then any discount over this percentage will be taxable. The discount must be available to all employees on a non-discriminatory basis. You can also offer up to a 20 percent tax-free discount on services.

Finally, a corporation, unlike a sole proprietorship or a partnership, can deduct charitable contributions up to 10 percent of its taxable income. Contributions in excess of this limitation can be carried over and deducted for up to five succeeding years, subject to certain limitations. Your corporation thus gives you the opportunity, unavailable to the sole proprietor or partnership, to support a charity or cause with tax-deductible business dollars.

Chapter 5. FORMING YOUR OWN MICHIGAN CORPORATION

If you have carefully read the preceding chapters and have decided that you are one of the many individuals who can benefit from the corporate form of business, you are now ready to learn about the procedure for setting up your own for-profit Michigan corporation.[1]

CORPORATE NAME

The first step in organizing your profit corporation is the choice of a name for your business which you like and which complies with state law. The Michigan statutes specify that your corporate name must contain either the word "corporation," "incorporated," "company," or "limited," or an abbreviation of one of these words ("corp.," "inc.," "co.," or "ltd."). Also, the name you select shall be distinguishable from all of the following: (1) that of another profit corporation (domestic or foreign) authorized to do business in Michigan, (2) that of a nonprofit Michigan corporation, or (3) that

of any Michigan domestic limited partnership or foreign limited partnership.

If you are presently running a business in the state as a sole proprietor or partner, you can use the same business name for your corporation as you presently have by just adding "Inc.," provided that another corporation is not now operating in Michigan under the same name. Even if the name you choose for your corporation is your own name, you still will not be able to use it if it turns out that someone is already doing business in Michigan under that name, unless you modify it in some way in order to clearly distinguish your business name from the other person's (Sorry, Mr. Ford in Saline.)

The P. Gaines Co. publishes a helpful book on selecting names for use in commerce: *Naming Your Business and Its Products and Services: How to Create Effective Trade Names, Trademarks, and Service Marks to Attract Customers, Protect Your Good Will and Reputation, and Stay Out of Court.* Every business, whether a corporation, a partnership, or a sole

---

1   If you are considering forming a professional service corporation as a doctor, dentist, engineer, etc., we suggest that you read this chapter first, then Chapter 6, which deals specifically with the Michigan professional service corporation. Also see Chapter 7, regarding the Michigan nonprofit corporation.

proprietorship, has to have a business name under which it conducts its affairs. In the event you do incorporate, it is important to realize that even though the business name you select for your company is approved by the Michigan Department of Commerce, this is no guarantee of the legality of the use of the name from the standpoint of trademark law. You may still be sued by an incorporated or unincorporated company in Michigan or in another state if the name chosen is the same as, or deceptively similar to, that of the other company's. The use of your family surname as your business name, furthermore, is often the worst possible choice, for several reasons. See the ad in the back of this book for additional information about this publication. *Naming Your Business and Its Products and Services* fully explains these and other significant issues in the business name selection process, whether that of a trade name, trademark, or service mark.

In addition, your company name cannot falsely imply professional affiliation or mislead in other ways. "Bank," "Industrial Bank," "Deposit," "Surety," "Security," "Trust," "Trust Company," and similar terms cannot ordinarily be part of your corporate name unless the corporation will actually be a bank, for example. Likewise, "Architect," "Landscape Architect," "Engineer," "Surveyor," and similar terms may only be used by professional service corporations which have complied with the requirements of the state board of registration of that profession as well as all applicable statutory provisions.

The name of the corporation need not be in the English language, provided that it is written in English letters or Arabic or Roman numerals.

Since you have to include the name of your corporation in the Articles of Incorporation which you file with the Department of Commerce, you may want to reserve the name you have decided on in advance. You can submit to the Department a written application requesting the use of a specified name as the name of your corporation (along with a ten-dollar filing fee). A copy of the form which you may use to reserve a corporate name is included in the back of this book in Appendix E. If the name specified in your application is available, you will be given the exclusive right to use it as the name of your corporation until the end of the fourth full calendar month following the month in which the application is filed (the reservation is also renewable).

If you are in a hurry to incorporate, the quickest procedure is to ask for a telephone confirmation of the availability of a particular name by calling 1-900-740-0031 [cost of $1.50 per minute]. Although a telephone check is a reliable indication in most cases, it does not absolutely guarantee the availability of a particular name which is cleared in this fashion. The Corporation Division reserves the right to make its final decision on the matter when a name reservation request has been approved or Articles of Incorporation have been filed.

As a necessary precaution, do not have business stationery or customized stock certificates printed or make other commitments to a name until the Articles of Incorporation have been filed, approved, and returned to you.

To save time, it may be a good idea to either reserve your name in advance or at least have a preliminary name check via phone. Otherwise, your Articles will be returned to you unfiled if the name you have chosen has already been taken, and you will have to refile again under another name . . . and again . . . and again, until you hit on a name that isn't currently being used. A little foresight and advance planning will eliminate these potential delays.

THE ARTICLES OF INCORPORATION

In order to obtain corporate status, you will now need to fill out and mail to the Department of Commerce one original copy (photocopied signatures not acceptable) of your Articles of Incorporation. This form is simple to complete in most cases. A copy of this form is available in Appendix A in the back of this book. If the form has already been removed or you have a library edition of this book whose forms are not of the tear-out variety, additional copies can be obtained by writing the Michigan Department of Commerce, Corporation and Securities Bureau, Corporation Division, PO Box 30054, Lansing, Michigan 48909 or phoning (517) 334-6206. When completing the form, which must be filled out in the English language (with the exception of foreign corpora-

tions), you should either type or print clearly in black ink all information.

Following is a sample Articles of Incorporation. Article One, the name of the corporation, we have already discussed. Be sure to consult our publication, *Naming Your Business and Its Products and Services*, before making your final name selection, to alert you to the legal pitfalls of a poorly chosen moniker and the potential rewards of an effective and legally defensible commercial name (see the ad in the back of this book for details on this publication). Assuming you have found an available name to your liking, you can fill it in here.

Article Two pertains to the purpose of the corporation. This article is already filled in on the form with a general purpose clause which most Michigan corporations can use as is without changing or amending in any way.

It is important to note that a general purpose clause such as this may *not* be used for nonprofit corporations (see Chapter 7), professional service corporations (see Chapter 6), and educational corporations (such as schools or colleges), whose purposes must be stated in compliance with all requirements of Sections 450.170 to 450.177 of the Michigan Compiled Laws of 1948. In most other cases, it is no longer necessary or even advisable to enumerate the specific types of business activities you are incorporating. By making this clause as broad as possible, you allow the future possibility of entering into related or even totally unrelated business activities, without the necessity of having to organize another corporation for that specific purpose or to amend the Articles of Incorporation of your existing business. Although today you are operating a shoe store, tomorrow you may meet someone in the scuba diving business and decide to pursue a whole new line. There are legal advantages to general purpose clauses as well, as in the case of an *ultra vires* lawsuit brought by a dissenting shareholder.[2]

Article Three concerns the issue of stock. According to our recommendation in Chapter 2, you would normally issue stock of no-par value, with the maximum number of authorized shares available under Michigan law (60,000) for the minimum filing fee ($60 total). Regarding the question of "common" vs. "preferred" stock, as noted previously, preferred stock is so named because shareholders of this type of stock receive their dividends first, before all other classes of stock, at a fixed rate of return. Common stock is paid after preferred, at a variable rate depending on the current profitability of the corporation. If the corporation is dissolved, preferred stockholders also would receive preferential treatment over common stockholders in the division of the corporate assets. Many publicly traded corporations listed on the New York and American Stock Exchanges have both preferred and common stock, but small, privately held corporations usually have no need to issue preferred stock.

Even certain small corporations may wish at some point to issue two classes of common stock, one voting and the other non-voting, however, as in the case of some family corporations who want to keep control of the corporation within the hands of several (or even one) family member(s), while giving other family members shares of dividend-paying stock. If you decide to have different classes of stock, the rights of each class concerning voting privileges, dividends, and so on will have to be decided and indicated in part 2 of Article Three. Since there are a number of different rights, preferences, and limitations assignable to stock, legal consultation is advisable if you wish to have two or more classes of stock. Also, you should check with the Michigan Division of Securities if you propose to authorize more than one class of stock, to be sure the wording of your stock provisions meets their approval.

As previously noted, you can authorize up to 60,000 shares of stock for the minimum filing fee ($60 total--the one-time incorporation fee of $10 plus a franchise tax of $50). You should, therefore, authorize the maximum number allowable (60,000) but issue only the number needed to capitalize your corporation initially. If you plan to start up your company with $10,000 in assets, you might issue 2,000 no par-value shares worth $5 each, for example.

You will note that there is no place on the Articles of Incorporation form to indicate

---

2   An *ultra vires* act is one in which a corporate officer or director has exceeded his authority as granted by the Articles of Incorporation or corporate bylaws.

the value of *issued* shares, only the value of authorized ones.) In the future, you may wish to issue additional shares in order to add more capital to your business. You may do so by purchasing additional shares yourself or by selling shares to other investors. As long as you do not issue more than the original number authorized in your Articles of Incorporation (60,000, according to our recommendation), you will not need to report these transactions to the state. If you issue 2,000 shares in the above example, you will have a whopping 58,000 additional shares that can be issued at some future date, if need be.

Any amount of capital (or none) in cash, property, accounts receivable, inventories, etc. may be initially put into your business when you incorporate. We do recommend beginning with enough start-up capital in your corporation to take care of foreseeable short-term expenses, although you do not have to specify the amount in the Articles.

You don't want to overcapitalize your corporation, on the other hand, since you will more quickly reach the ceiling set by the IRS for accumulated earnings. At that point, money paid to stockholders will usually take the form of dividends, subject to the "double tax" discussed previously. This is generally not a concern for firms with $50,000 or less in start-up capital.

An aside: one good way to keep from tying up more capital than necessary when you incorporate is to provide part of the initial seed money in the form of a short-term loan to the corporation. The corporation need not pay you interest on the loan as long as it is truly of short-term duration, say, three months or less and is not more than about $3,000. If it turns out that the corporation needs this loan money for an extended period of time to stay afloat, however, you may run into problems with the IRS in later taking this money out of the corporation.[3] To avoid running afoul of the ever-watchful authorities, larger start-up loans for longer periods of time should carry an interest charge at market rates, which is a deductible expense for the corporation.

Article Four asks for information about the registered office and the resident agent of the corporation. The purpose of this information is to provide for public record a legal mailing address and contact person to receive corporate mailings from the Department of Commerce, as well as legal documents (summons, subpoenas) in connection with any lawsuits that might arise against the corporation. The resident agent must be a resident of Michigan and would ordinarily be one of the corporate directors. The registered office must be located in Michigan, and its actual street address given (post office box alone not acceptable). In theory, you could authorize anyone residing in Michigan to act as your

---

3   The IRS may argue that this money is not actually a loan at all but equity capital needed for day-to-day business operations. Therefore, the return of this money would be considered for tax purposes as a dividend and would be taxable to the recipient.

C&S 500 (Rev. 2-92)

MICHIGAN DEPARTMENT OF COMMERCE — CORPORATION AND SECURITIES BUREAU

Date Received			**(FOR BUREAU USE ONLY)**

Name

Address

City   State   ZIP Code

EFFECTIVE DATE:

DOCUMENT WILL BE RETURNED TO NAME AND ADDRESS INDICATED ABOVE

CORPORATION IDENTIFICATION NUMBER

ARTICLES OF INCORPORATION
For use by Domestic Profit Corporations
(Please read information and instructions on the last page)

Pursuant to the provisions of Act 284, Public Acts of 1972, the undersigned corporation executes the following Articles:

ARTICLE I

The name of the corporation is:

WANDA GOLD ENTERPRISES, INC.

ARTICLE II

The purpose or purposes for which the corporation is formed is to engage in any activity within the purposes for which corporations may be formed under the Business Corporation Act of Michigan.

ARTICLE III

The total authorized shares:
1. Common Shares______60,000______

   Preferred Shares______

2. A statement of all or any of the relative rights, preferences and limitations of the shares of each class is as follows:

ARTICLE IV

1. The address of the registered office is:

920 Moose Road _Dexter_ , Michigan _48130_
(Street Address)   (City)   (ZIP Code)

2. The mailing address of the registered office if different from the registered office address:

same , Michigan _______
(P.O. Box)   (City)   (ZIP Code)

3. The name of the resident agent at the registered office is: _Wanda Gold_

ARTICLE V

The name(s) and address(es) of the incorporator(s) is (are) as follows:

Name	Residence or Business Address
Wanda Gold	920 Moose Rd, Dexter, Michigan 48130

ARTICLE VI (Optional. Delete if not applicable)

When a compromise or arrangement or a plan of reorganization of this corporation is proposed between this corporation and its creditors or any class of them or between this corporation and its shareholders or any class of them, a court of equity jurisdiction within the state, on application of this corporation or of a creditor or shareholder thereof, or on application of a receiver appointed for the corporation, may order a meeting of the creditors or class of creditors or of the shareholders or class of shareholders to be affected by the proposed compromise or arrangement or reorganization, to be summoned in such manner as the court directs. If a majority in number representing 3/4 in value of the creditors or class of creditors, or of the shareholders or class of shareholders to be affected by the proposed compromise or arrangement or a reorganization, agree to a compromise or arrangement or a reorganization of this corporation as a consequence of the compromise or arrangement, the compromise or arrangement and the reorganization, if sanctioned by the court to which the application has been made, shall be binding on all the creditors or class of creditors, or on all the shareholders or class of shareholders and also on this corporation.

ARTICLE VII (Optional. Delete if not applicable)

Any action required or permitted by the Act to be taken at an annual or special meeting of shareholders may be taken without a meeting, without prior notice, and without a vote, if consents in writing, setting forth the action so taken, are signed by the holders of outstanding shares having not less than the minimum number of votes that would be necessary to authorize or take the action at a meeting at which all shares entitled to vote on the action were present and voted. The written consents shall bear the date of signature of each shareholder who signs the consent. No written consents shall be effective to take the corporate action referred to unless, within 60 days after the record date for determining shareholders entitled to express consent to or to dissent from a proposal without a meeting, written consents signed by a sufficient number of shareholders to take the action are delivered to the corporation. Delivery shall be to the corporation's registered office, its principal place of business, or an officer or agent of the corporation having custody of the minutes of the proceedings of its shareholders. Delivery made to a corporation's registered office shall be by hand or by certified or registered mail, return receipt requested.

Prompt notice of the taking of the corporate action without a meeting by less than unanimous written consent shall be given to shareholders who have not consented in writing.

Use space below for additional Articles or for continuation of previous Articles. Please identify any Article being continued or added. Attach additional pages if needed.

As provided in the Michigan Business Corporation Act, this corporation (Wanda Gold Enterprises, Inc.) elects to have cumulative voting procedures.

I (We), the incorporator(s) sign my (our) name(s) this ___2nd___ day of ___December___ , 19 _92_ .

Wanda Gold

Name of person or organization
remitting fees:

Wanda Gold

Preparer's name and business
telephone number:

Wanda Gold

(313) 999-0201

INFORMATION AND INSTRUCTIONS

1. The articles of incorporation cannot be filed until this form, or a comparable document, is submitted.

2. Submit one original copy of this document. Upon filing, a microfilm copy will be prepared for the records of the Corporation and Securities Bureau. The original copy will be returned to the address appearing in the box on the front as evidence of filing.

   Since this document must be microfilmed, it is important that the filing be legible. Documents with poor black and white contrast, or otherwise illegible, will be rejected.

3. This document is to be used pursuant to the provisions of Act 284, P.A. of 1972, by one or more persons for the purpose of forming a domestic profit corporation.

4. Article I—The corporate name of a domestic profit corporation is required to contain one of the following words or abbreviations: "Corporation", "Company", "Incorporated", "Limited", "Corp.", "Co.", "Inc.", or "Ltd.".

5. Article II—State, in general terms, the character of the particular business to be carried on. Under section 202(b) of the Act, it is sufficient to state substantially, alone or with specifically enumerated purposes, that the corporation may engage in any activity within the purposes for which corporations may be formed under the Act. The Act requires, however, that educational corporations state their specific purposes.

6. Article IV—A post office box may not be designated as the address of the registered office.

7. Article V—The Act requires one or more incorporators. Educational corporations are required to have three (3) incorporators. The address(es) should include a street number and name (or other designation), city and state.

8. The duration of the corporation should be stated in the articles only if the duration is not perpetual.

9. This document is effective on the date approved and filed by the Bureau. A later effective date, no more than 90 days after the date of delivery, may be stated as an additional article.

10. The articles must be signed in ink by each incorporator. The names of the incorporators as set out in article V should correspond with the signatures.

11. FEES: (Make remittance payable to the State of Michigan). Include corporation name on check or money order.
    Franchise fee: first 60,000 authorized shares or portion thereof... $50.00
    each additional 20,000 authorized shares or portion thereof $30.00
    Non-Refundable filing fee $10.00
    Total minimum fees $60.00

12. Mail form and fee to:
    Michigan Department of Commerce
    Corporation and Securities Bureau
    Corporation Division
    P.O. Box 30054
    6546 Mercantile Way
    Lansing, MI 48909
    Telephone: (517) 334-6302

resident agent, such as an attorney or a friend. If you are the sole owner-operator of the proposed corporation, you can simply fill in your own name as resident agent and your business address as the address of the registered office. Any changes in the address of the registered office or the name of the resident agent at a later date must, of course, be filed with the Department of Commerce. Failure to file such information may result in the dissolution of the corporation's Articles.

Article Five requests the name(s) and address(es) of the incorporator(s). Either a residence or business address may be provided, consisting of a street number and name, city, and state.

Two optional articles, Articles Six and Seven, are also included on the form. These pertain, respectively, to the manner in which the corporation may be reorganized and to actions by stockholders taken without a meeting. These may be deleted if desired by crossing them out; in most cases, it would be advantageous to keep them. A provision for corporate actions without a meeting are also included in the bylaws in Appendix B.

In addition to these articles which must be filled in, additional space is provided on the form to specify various additional points in your Articles of Incorporation. Since the "life" of a corporation is assumed to be perpetual in Michigan unless stated otherwise, you may specify a fixed period for your corporation in this space. Such a fixed-life corporation might be appropriate in the case of a corporation organized for the purpose of conducting a political campaign, for instance. If you wish your corporation to have cumulative voting (explained in Chapter 2, pages 29-30), this should be specified here also.

Another major area often covered by additional articles is that pertaining to what is generally termed a "close corporation agreement" (although Michigan law makes no distinction between this type of corporation and a regular corporation). The main purpose of a close corporation option is to allow the shareholder(s) of a corporation to agree upon provisions regulating any aspect of the internal affairs of the corporation. The running of the corporation under a so-called "shareholders' agreement" (without a board of directors and other formalities) is permitted and may be specified here. The placing of restrictions upon the transfer of stock to outsiders is also allowed. See Appendix E for a list of the various options available under a close corporation agreement. Small or even one-man or one-woman corporations which wish to dispense with much of the formality of larger corporations may wish to adopt some type of close corporation agreement. In one-person corporations, the elimination of the board of directors is frequently a necessity, for instance. It may be a good idea to maintain a minimum of formality by having traditional offices, that of a president and a secretary-treasurer at least—even if the same person holds both positions. Those completely informal corporations which dispense with both corporate officers and directors by means of a shareholders' agreement may encounter difficulties in getting bank loans, dealing with the IRS, and so on.

Finally, the copy of the completed Articles of Incorporation must be dated and signed by the incorporator(s). The individuals whose signatures appear here should also be the same ones named in Article Five above.

On the back of the form is a space for you to indicate the name of the person or organization remitting fees and a space to show the preparer's name and business telephone. If you are the sole incorporator and filled out the form yourself, you would include your name in both these spaces.

The completed Articles of Incorporation are filed with the Corporation Division of the Department of Commerce, along with the appropriate fee. Michigan for-profit corporations pay a minimum fee of $60, provided that they have authorized capital stock totaling 60,000 shares or less (a $10 filing fee and a minimum franchise fee of $50). Since the franchise fee is tied to the number of shares authorized, additional payment will be due at the rate of $30 for each additional 20,000 shares authorized (or portion thereof). Most small business corporations which do not plan to make a public offering of their stock will be perfectly well off with the maximum number of capital shares allowable (60,000) for the minimum filing fee. Payment of the total fees ($60 in most cases) may be made by money order, cashier's check, or personal check.

TRANSFERRING ASSETS AND LIABILITIES TO YOUR NEW CORPORATION

When you are ready to start business as a corporation, if you are beginning from scratch, you will simply turn over the assets which you are offering to the corporation as start-up capital in exchange for stock. The actual transfer procedure will be discussed below under "Issuing Shares of Stock."

If you already have a going business (sole proprietorship or partnership), the transfer will be a bit more complicated, since you have the option of transferring liabilities as well as assets. Legal counsel is advisable to assure the best arrangement tax-wise in your individual circumstances. Generally speaking, the total amount of liabilities transferred (accounts payable is one type of liability, for example) should not exceed the total amount of assets transferred (accounts receivable, inventories, etc.). Since the individual is personally relieved of his liabilities when he forms a corporation and transfers the debts to it, the amount of the net debt assumed by the company is considered a taxable benefit. The IRS will thus regard the excess of liabilities over assets as a cash payment which is taxable to the individual. To be on the safe side, you can always balance your assets and liabilities by donating some personal assets to the corporation, such as a typewriter, a computer, a file cabinet, a desk, and so on. Of course, if the assets transferred are greater than the liabilities, there is no problem—only the reverse imbalance will result in punitive taxes. If you transfer the entire business to the corporation, including inventory, capital assets, accounts payable and receivable, the IRS will not tax the uncollected receivables as long as you meet one test. You have to receive control of at least 80 percent of the new corporation (including a minimum of 80 percent of voting stock as well as 80 percent of non-voting stock, if applicable).

In Chapter 1, the possibility of taking back only a portion of the value of your appraised business in stock was mentioned. By receiving only $40,000 in stock in partial payment for a business worth, say, $200,000, the balance of $160,000 is treated as a loan from you to the corporation. The corporation consequently issues you a note for $160,000 and pays you back this sum, plus interest, over the term of years you specify in the note. Such an arrangement has the decided advantage of producing mostly tax-free income to you— only the *interest portion* will be taxable. The rest will be treated by the IRS as a return of principal, which is nontaxable.

You also have the option of shutting down your sole proprietorship or partnership, so that you commence business as a corporation on a fresh basis. It may take several months or more to wind down your old business, but you need not wait until this process is totally completed before starting your corporation. Just be sure to keep business records of the proprietorship or partnership separate from those of the corporation, for both tax and legal purposes. You will also want to notify creditors in writing of the dissolution of the prior business and of the existence of the new corporation. This can be accomplished with a form letter which might accompany your regular business advertisements.

ORDERING CORPORATE RECORDS BOOK, SEAL AND STOCK CERTIFICATES

The Michigan Business Corporation Act requires that every Michigan corporation keep minutes of the meetings of its shareholders and board of directors as well as a record of shareholders, giving the names and addresses of all shareholders, the number, class, and series of shares held by each, and the dates when they became shareholders of record. Minutes may be kept in written form or in any other form capable of being converted into written form within a reasonable time.

You may purchase a fancy records book from a stationery store, but any three-ring binder will serve the purpose. We offer a reasonably priced and attractive Black Beauty Corporate Outfit which includes 50 blank sheets of rag content 20-lb. bond Minute Paper as well as a binder for minutes, corporate bylaws, and stock records. Please refer to the ad in the back of this book for additional information about this individually customized corporate outfit.

Michigan law does not require you to have a corporate seal, but many corporations do use one. You may be asked for the seal imprint on formal agreements such as the application for the corporate bank accounts, bank loan papers, and lease agreements, although its use, technically speaking, is optional. A seal can be ordered from most stationery stores at a cost of approximately $20 to $25. The corporate kit advertised in the back of this book also contains a corporate seal. The corporate seal is circular and contains the name of the corporation exactly as filed with the Department of Commerce, the name of the state (Michigan), the words "Corporate SEAL," and the year of incorporation.

While the Michigan statutes no longer require that certificates signed by officials of the corporation represent shares of stock of Michigan for-profit corporations, we do recommend their use for small corporations as an effective means of organizing the corporation. The certificate is simply a concrete representation of one's capital holdings in a corporation. A certificate may be used to represent more than one share of stock. Each certificate shall state:

1. That the corporation is organized under the laws of the state of Michigan
2. The name of the person to whom issued
3. The number of shares represented by the certificate
4. If the shares of the corporation are classified, the designation of the class of shares, and the designation of the series, if any, which such certificate represents
5. If the corporation is authorized to issue more than one class or series of shares, the designation, relative rights, preferences and limitations of the shares of each class or series of shares authorized to be issued, which shall be set forth on the front or back of the certificate, or a statement to the effect that the corporation will furnish to a shareholder all such information upon request
6. If the Articles of Incorporation contain a provision authorized by section 450.1463 (1) providing that there shall not be a board of directors, or any other form of "shareholders' agreement" whereby part or all the management of the corporation shall be conducted by the shareholders instead of a board of directors, the existence of this provision shall be noted conspicuously on the face of every certificate for shares issued by the corporation

It is standard practice for corporations to imprint their stock certificates with their corporate seal. Stock certificates may be purchased from many of the larger stationery stores. The Black Beauty Corporate Outfit which we offer contains 20 attractive certificates which are custom printed with the corporate name, state, officers' titles, and capitalization. Or you may choose to use the tear-out stock certificates included in the back of this book.

PREORGANIZATION SUBSCRIPTION AGREEMENT

If you are a one-man band, then a subscription agreement will not be necessary. If other shareholders will be involved in setting up the corporation, however, you may wish to have them sign a "preorganization subscription agreement." This agreement is legally binding in the state of Michigan, provided that it is in writing and signed by the subscriber. A subscription for shares of a corporation to be organized is irrevocable and may be accepted by the corporation for a period of six months, unless otherwise provided by the subscription agreement or unless all the subscribers consent to its revocation. Once Articles of Incorporation are filed with the Department of Commerce, all subscribers for shares shall be deemed to be shareholders of the corporation. The board of directors determines when subscriptions for shares are to be paid (normally immediately following the first board of directors meeting). The call for payment must be uniform for all the shareholders of the same class. In the case of default, the corporation may proceed to collect the amount due in the same manner as any debt owed to the corporation. It may also rescind the subscription, sell the shares to a third party, and sue the defaulter for breach of contract. A sample subscription agreement follows hereafter. See Appendix E for a copy of this agreement which you can adopt for your own corporation. If you have more subscribers than you can fit on one sheet, you can make as many additional copies of this form as necessary.

PREPARING THE BYLAWS

You are now ready to prepare the bylaws for your corporation, which may contain any provision for the regulation or management of the affairs of the corporation that are not inconsistent with law or the Articles of Incorporation. The initial bylaws of a Michigan corporation shall be adopted by its incorporators, its shareholders, or its board. The shareholders or the board may amend or repeal the bylaws or adopt new bylaws, unless power to do so is reserved exclusively to the shareholders by the Articles of Incorporation. The shareholders may prescribe in the bylaws that any bylaw made by them shall not be altered or repealed by the board.

We provide in Appendix B in the back of this book a set of bylaws which you can modify for your corporation's use by filling in the blanks and making minor alterations. If you are having an attorney prepare your incorporation, be sure to ask if he is using a "kit" with standard bylaws; if not, find out why, because you will pay dearly if he or she has to draw up customized bylaws (in most cases, they are unnecessary). First, indicate the name of your corporation at the top of the page. In Article I, write in the name of the city/village/township (cross out the ones that don't apply) and the county where the principal executive office of the corporation is located. In Article II, Section 2, indicate the date and time (5th of May at 6 P.M., for example) on which the annual shareholders' meeting is to be held. This will be the same date as the regular directors' meeting (Article III, Section 5). Often this date is set shortly before or after the close of the corporation's fiscal year, so that both the previous year and the coming year's business can be discussed. If you want your fiscal year to coincide with the calendar year, however (beginning on January 1 and ending on December 31), you will want to hold your annual meeting close to the date on which your corporation is initially organized. In Article III, Section 2, indicate the number of directors of the corporation. Read through the bylaws to familiarize yourself with the contents. We

<h1 style="text-align:center">PREORGANIZATION SUBSCRIPTION AGREEMENT</h1>

We, the undersigned, severally subscribe to the number of shares set opposite our respective names of capital stock of a proposed corporation, to be known as *Wanda Gold Enterprises Inc* or by any other name that the incorporators may select, and to be incorporated in the State of Michigan. We agree to pay the sum of $ *10.00* per each share subscribed.

This subscription shall not be binding on the undersigned unless subscriptions in the aggregate amount of $ *10,000.00* for shares of said corporation have been procured on or before the *2nd* day of *December* , 19 *92* .

All subscriptions hereto shall be payable at such time or times as the board of directors of said corporation may determine and shall be paid in cash, except as hereinafter indicated. (If any of the subscriptions are to be paid by transferring property to the corporation, a description of the property shall be attached hereto.)

Date	Name and Address	Number of Shares	Amount Subscribed
11-27-92	Wanda Gold 920 Moose Road. Dexter, Michigan 48130	500	$5,000.00
11-30-92	Junior Gold 912 Virtue Blvd Dexter, Michigan 48130	(250)	$2,500.00
12/1/92	Sissy Gold 814 Persimmon Lane Saline, Michigan 48176	250	$2,500.0

will assume that your bylaws will be approved at the first shareholders' meeting, although, as noted above, they may be approved by the incorporators or directors (or all three!).

FIRST MEETING OF SHAREHOLDERS

After the corporation has been organized and the Articles of Incorporation filed with the Department of Commerce and returned to you approved, the first meeting of the shareholders can be convened.[4] It is advisable to have each shareholder sign a waiver of notice form (included in Appendix C), in order to dispense with formal notice requirements. If there is more than one shareholder, a chairman who will preside at the meeting and a secretary who will keep minutes should be appointed. Minutes of this meeting which may be adopted for most corporations are in Appendix C.

The meeting should be advised that the Articles of Incorporation have been filed and approved. A resolution to approve the Articles and to accept their filing should be made. If a subscription agreement has been used, it should be read and formally approved also.

The chairman informs the shareholders of the number of directors to be elected (if applicable). Nominations are accepted and voted on. The Michigan statutes, as mentioned previously, provide for the option of cumulative voting if the Articles of Incorporation so provide. As explained in Chapter 2, under cumulative voting procedures the number of votes each shareholder is entitled to is determined by multiplying the number of shares he holds by the number of directors to be elected. In the case of the three-shareholder corporation of Wanda, Junior, and Giesela Gold, Wanda would have 300 votes and Junior and Giesela 150 votes each, if Wanda holds 100 shares of stock and the other two have 50 shares each and three directors are to be elected. Each may cast all of his votes for one nominee or divide them among several candidates in any proportion desired. The purpose of cumulative voting is to give minority shareholders greater voting power and representation than would otherwise be the case.

After the election of directors, the corporate bylaws are presented for approval, if the initial bylaws are to be approved by the shareholders. A majority of the voting power represented by the shareholders will constitute approval. After the meeting of shareholders is adjourned, the directors hold their first meeting (assuming that your corporation will have directors).

---

4   As already pointed out, the Michigan Business Corporation Act (section 450.1463) provides for the option of a shareholders' agreement whereby the corporate directors may be dispensed with and the business of the corporation conducted entirely by the shareholders.

FIRST MEETING OF THE BOARD OF DIRECTORS

The purpose of the first meeting of the board of directors is to elect officers, adopt the corporate seal and stock certificates, establish a fiscal year, decide on a bank or banks where the corporation will maintain accounts, and to make other types of resolutions. In the back of the book in Appendix D, you will find a set of corporate minutes which may be adopted for the first meeting of the board of directors. You may fill in the blanks with the pertinent information for your corporation and neatly cross out any resolutions that are not applicable to you.

We will go step by step through the first meeting of the board of directors and the preparation of the minutes of the meeting. First, you may tear out the "Waiver of Notice," which is the first form in Appendix D, and fill in the blanks, indicating the date, time, and place of the meeting and have all the directors sign it.

One of the directors is to be chosen chairman and to preside, while another director should be selected to act as secretary. The secretary will complete the first page of the minutes by filling in the time, place, and date of the meeting and the names of the directors present as well as any absentees. The names of the chairman and the secretary are to be shown in the spaces provided.

The meeting should be advised of the filing of the Articles of Incorporation and their approval by the Department of Commerce. The filing date should be recorded in the appropriate place in the minutes. The meeting thereafter acknowledges the adoption of the bylaws by the shareholders (if the Articles of Incorporation so provide).

An election of officers should be conducted. When completed, the permanent secretary and president will replace the temporary ones appointed previously. The names of the officers elect are shown in the spaces provided in the minutes. As discussed in Chapter 2 under "Officers," one person may hold more than one or even all the offices, if the Articles or the bylaws so provide.

When the resolution concerning the corporate seal has been read and passed, the secretary should make an impression of the seal in the space provided in the right-hand margin. A resolution to adopt the type of stock certificate to be issued by the corporation follows next.

The location of the principal executive office of the corporation should next be entered in the spaces provided.

The directors must establish a fiscal year for the corporation. It is simplest to have your fiscal year coincide with the calendar year (beginning January 1 and ending December 31). You also have the option of having your fiscal year be another twelve-month period ending on the last day of a month other than December (May 1 to April 30, for example). Another possibility allowed by the IRS is to have your fiscal year end on the same day of the week in the same month each year, for instance, the last Friday in June. In this case, your fiscal year will have 52 weeks during some years and 53 weeks in other years. Since various tax and accounting questions are connected to the establishment of a fiscal year, you may want to consult a tax adviser about this issue. Fill in the information concerning the fiscal year in the minutes.

The choice of a bank or banks for corporate accounts should be made and shown in the designated place. If you wish more than one officer to endorse checks, you should insert a separate resolution to this effect.

A resolution approving your "Medical Care Reimbursement Plan" should be presented and adopted, if you wish your corporation to pay the medical expenses of the employees and their dependents. Be sure to consult with a tax adviser to assure the tax-free status of this and other corporate fringe benefit plans (see the discussion in Chapter 4, under "Medical Reimbursement Plans," pages 43-44). A copy of one type of model plan is included in Appendix E.

The next resolution about compensation of officers requires that the officers' salaries be decided upon and shown in the appropriate blanks.

If you wish to elect Subchapter S treatment for your corporation, then a resolution to this effect should be made and included in the minutes. (See Chapter 8, "The S Corporation)." We have included this optional resolution in the minutes. Cross it out if your corporation does not make this election.

Resolutions are also included in the minutes regarding the qualification of common stock as 1244 stock. The purpose of these resolutions is to allow the stockholders of the corporation the benefit of treating losses from the sale, exchange, or worthlessness of their stock as "ordinary" instead of "capital" losses. Since ordinary losses are generally fully deductible whereas long-term capital losses are only 50 percent deductible, it is advantageous to have your stock treated as 1244 stock.

Resolutions concerning the sale and issuance of capital stock are also normally in order. You may fill in the blank showing the number of shares authorized in the Articles of Incorporation. Shares of stock issued for cash are easily entered in the minutes by indicating in the blanks the number of shares purchased and the price of each share. In the case of shares issued for property, the number of shares exchanged for property and the price per share as well as a description of the property are to be shown in the next resolution.

If you are transferring the assets and liabilities of a going business to the corporation in exchange for stock, then you will need to complete the next two resolutions as well. Technically speaking, even if you are the sole owner of a proprietorship and are transferring this business to the corporation, a "Bill of Sale Agreement" should be executed (see Appendix E for a model of this form). The date of the offer of transfer of business, which details the assets and liabilities of the business being transferred, and the fair market value of the business should be indicated in the appropriate blanks.

Finally, the secretary will need to sign the last page of the minutes. A copy of the waiver of notice, a copy of the prepared minutes, a copy of the Articles of Incorporation, a sample copy of the corporation stock certificate (with the word "SPECIMEN" written across the face), a copy of the bank depository resolution form, and any other applicable forms should be placed in the corporate records book. Stock certificates and stubs may be placed in a separate binder or in a special section of the same binder as the other corporate records. Minutes of future meetings of shareholders and directors and all other documents pertaining to the corporation such as loan agreement forms and other legal papers should be filed with the corporate records upon receipt. The corporate records book is required by law to be kept at the principal executive office at all times. In the event of an audit by the IRS or a lawsuit, your corporate records may be subject to close scrutiny. No matter how small your corporation, if you do not keep proper records, you may be subject to various legal and tax penalties.

ISSUING SHARES OF STOCK

Once the first meeting of the board of directors is concluded, stock certificates can now be issued in exchange for cash or the assets of a going business. If you sell stock to more than 10 persons (a husband, wife and children living as a family, a corporation, and a partnership are each counted as one "person"), you will need to contact the Securities Division, since you may be required to register the stock offering and pay a fee.

There are additional criteria that must be met before the stock issuance of your corporation can qualify for exemption from registration requirements: no commission can be paid for soliciting any prospective subscriber, the stock cannot be advertised unless the advertisement has been reviewed and no objection made by the Securities Division, and the seller must reasonably believe that all the buyers in this state are purchasing for investment. [5]

Each share certificate can represent any number of shares of stock, the number of shares to be indicated in the upper right-hand corner of the certificate. In addition, each certificate can be issued to more than one person if desired, in the case of husband and wife or other individuals who wish to hold stock jointly with rights of survivorship or as tenants in common or as tenants by the entireties. A sample stock certificate and instructions for filling it out follow hereafter.

---

[5] You can reach the Securities Division by telephone at (517) 334-6200; the mailing address is PO Box 30222, Lansing, Michigan 48909.

Instructions for Filling out Stock Certificates

First, fill out the stub portion of the stock certificates, which is either attached directly to the certificates or separate. The stubs are attached to the certificates in this book. The stock certificates bound into the back of this book have a stub that is folded under. After removing a certificate by tearing along the perforated line and unfolding the stub, it will appear attached to the certificate, on the left side. Detach the stub and fill it out as follows.

Concerning the certificate number to be supplied in the top center space, you will simply number consecutively each certificate to be issued, 1, 2,3, etc. (If you have more stockholders than the number of certificates in this book, you will need to purchase additional certificates, of course.) Be sure that the number on the stub matches the number on the face of the certificate. The stub numbered 1 will be the corporate record of the certificate numbered 1, issued to a particular stockholder, for instance.

Moving down the stub, next indicate the number of shares purchased by that individual and the name of the person to whom issued and fill in the date.

Leave the middle section, "From Whom Transferred," blank. This is used in the case of transfer of the certificate to a new owner.

At the bottom of the stub, you again fill in the certificate number, the number of shares, the date of issuance, and have the stockholder sign on the bottom line.

On the stock certificate proper, indicate the certificate number in the upper left-hand corner and the number of shares represented by the certificate in the upper right-hand corner. Fill in the name of the state in the space under the words "Incorporated Under the Laws of". The upper middle portion of the certificate has a large blank space in which to write the name of the corporation. In the body of the certificate, you may simply fill in the blanks for the owner's name and number of shares. The next blank can be used to indicate the par value of the stock ($10 each, for example). If you have issued no par-value stock, write "no par value" in the blank instead.

In the space for the name of the shareholder, you can, as noted, write in more than one name. If this is done, you would normally put in brackets after the names the type of joint ownership elected, for example: **Junior and Concha Gold (joint tenants in common)**

On the right side of the certificate outside the border, you can indicate that your stock issuance conforms with Section 1244 of the Internal Revenue Code for favorable tax treatment, allowing you to deduct corporate losses as an ordinary loss deduction on your personal income tax return (subject to certain limitations). If you choose to have your stock treated as 1244 Stock, you may type the following statement on this portion of the stock certificate:

THESE SHARES ARE ISSUED IN ACCORDANCE WITH SECTION 1244 OF THE INTERNAL REVENUE CODE

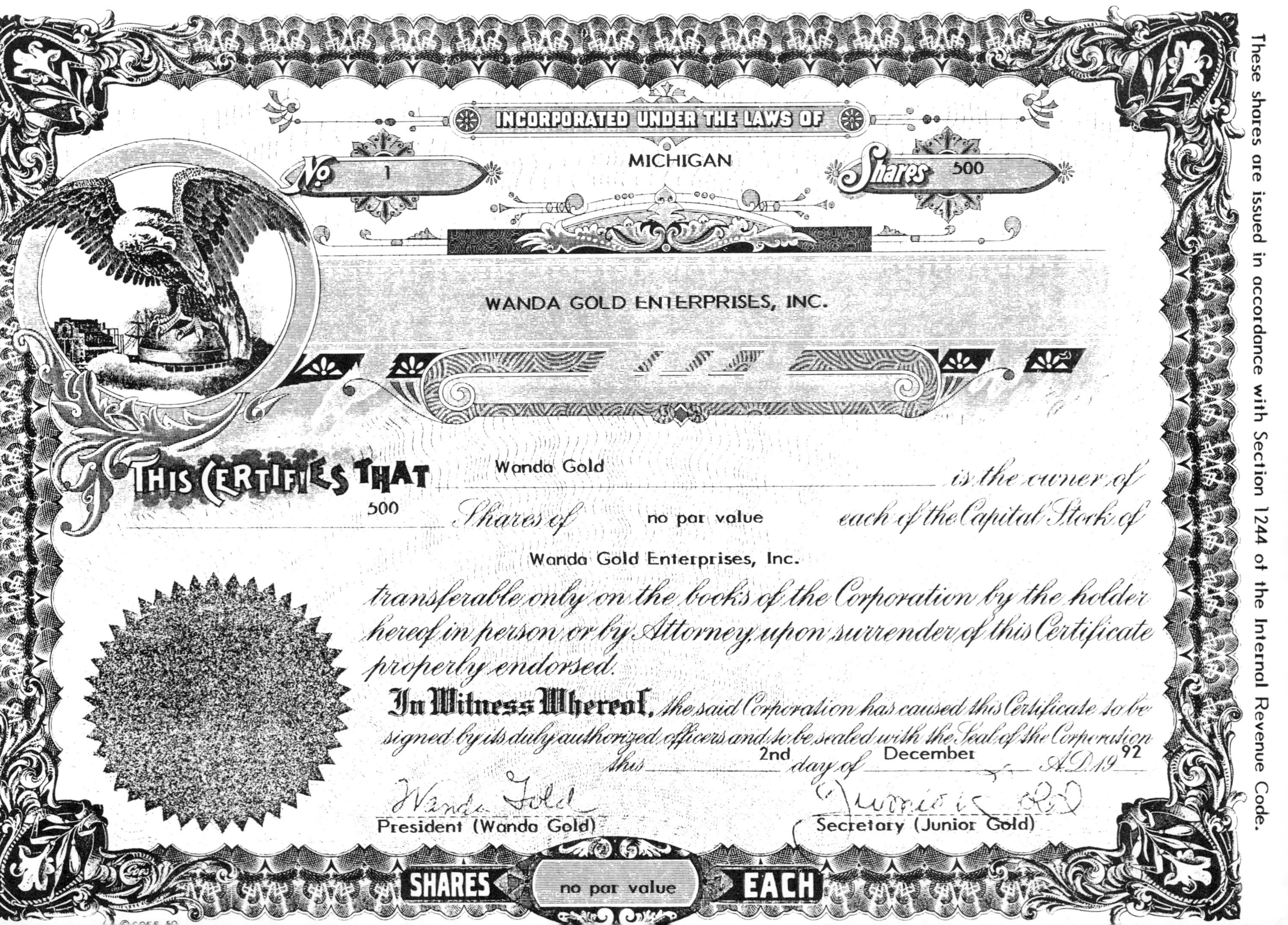

These shares are issued in accordance with Section 1244 of the Internal Revenue Code.
INCORPORATED UNDER THE LAWS OF
MICHIGAN
No. 1
Shares 500
WANDA GOLD ENTERPRISES, INC.
THIS CERTIFIES THAT
Wanda Gold
is the owner of
500
Shares of
no par value
each of the Capital Stock of
Wanda Gold Enterprises, Inc.
transferable only on the books of the Corporation by the holder hereof in person or by Attorney, upon surrender of this Certificate properly endorsed.
In Witness Whereof, the said Corporation has caused this Certificate to be signed by its duly authorized officers and to be sealed with the Seal of the Corporation this 2nd day of December A.D. 19 92
President (Wanda Gold)
Secretary (Junior Gold)
SHARES
no par value
EACH

An impression of the corporate seal may be made in the gold circular sunburst area at the bottom left side of the certificate.

The date of issuance should also be shown in the place provided. There is space at the bottom of the certificate to type in the names of the corporate officer(s), after each has signed in the appropriate spot.

Each shareholder is given a completed certificate in exchange for cash or the assets of a going business. Stock issued in exchange for cash should be paid for by personal check so that the shareholder will have proof of payment. It is recommended that receipts for cash payments also be issued by the corporation, showing the amount of money received, the check number, the name of the shareholder and the number of shares purchased, the name of the corporation, and the name of the treasurer, as well as the treasurer's signature.

A duplicate copy of each shareholder's receipt should be kept in the share certificates section of the corporate records book. Regarding stock issued in exchange for the assets of a going business, a copy of the signed and dated bill of sale (See Appendix E for this form) will provide documentation of this transaction.

EMPLOYER IDENTIFICATION NUMBER

As soon as possible after filing the Articles of Incorporation and selecting a fiscal year for your corporation, you should apply to the IRS for an Employer Identification Number (EIN). You may already have an EIN if you are in business as a sole proprietor. This one won't work, however. You will be required to obtain a new EIN as a corporation.

The form to file is an SS-4, Application for Employer Identification Number. You can phone your local IRS office and request an SS-4 by mail or pick one up in person. It will usually take 3 to 6 weeks after applying to receive your number.

If any forms, such as your application for a corporate bank account, ask for the EIN before it arrives, you can put down "number applied for," with the understanding that you will notify the appropriate authorities immediately upon receipt.

FILING AN ASSUMED NAME

There is one more procedure that may or may not apply to your newly formed corporation. Say you incorporate your business under the names of the principals, Unamuno, Grimmelshausen, and Horowitz, Inc. When you are ready to print business cards and stationery, have business signs painted, or run advertisements about your new company, you may have second thoughts about having chosen such a long, cumbersome name, so you decide to call yourselves UGH, Inc. for short.

You must file this "fictitious name" with the Department of Commerce. Request a copy of the Certificate of Assumed Name from the Department of Commerce and submit it with a $10 fee payment. The registration is good for 5 years, and may be renewed within 90 days of expiration (the corporation will automatically be notified of the impending expiration). Whenever the name under which you do business is different in some way from the one you originally filed when you incorporated, you must follow this procedure. If you operate under the exact corporate name, then it is, of course, not necessary to file an assumed name.

CORPORATE CHANGES

If you make mistakes of judgment in your original Articles of Incorporation which you later wish to correct, if you wish to change any provision(s) of the original Articles, change your corporate name, convert from a regular to a nonprofit corporation, or authorize additional shares of stock, if the address of your registered office changes, and so on, you must notify the Department of Commerce of these and similar changes. Contact the Department for the appropriate form and fee, ranging from $5 for an address change to $10 for amending your Articles of Incorporation.

Chapter 6. THE MICHIGAN PROFESSIONAL SERVICE CORPORATION

This chapter will point out certain general characteristics of professional service corporations and discuss specific Michigan laws governing their formation in this state. Professionals who desire to incorporate their practices are strongly advised to use the services of a lawyer.

Professional Liability

As noted in Chapter 1, the owner(s)-operator(s) of a Michigan professional service corporation cannot limit personal liability by means of the "corporate veil" like employees of regular corporations. Nevertheless, professionals who incorporate have more protection from liability than a partnership or sole proprietor.

Although the corporate form does not shield you from personal liability as a professional practitioner in the case of your own malpractice, it does limit your liability as a shareholder of the corporation. If your business goes bankrupt, the personal service corporation protects your personal assets from creditors in the same way that a regular corporation does. A professional service corporation also provides you with a degree of protection from malpractice on the part of your associates.

Fringe Benefits

Many of the same benefits exist for the professional corporation as for the regular for-profit corporation, such as the deductibility of medical and dental expenses and of premiums paid for medical, disability, and life insurance (up to $50,000 group-term coverage per employee), a $5,000 death benefit, free meals and lodgings furnished for the convenience of the corporation, deductible educational expenses up to $5,250 per employee, employee discounts on goods and services, free parking, group legal services plans, on-site physical fitness facilities, and deductible charitable contributions up to 10% of taxable income per year.

Limit on Business Activities

Your professional service corporation cannot engage in any business other than rendering those professional services specifically noted in its Articles of Incorporation, but it is permitted to own stocks, bonds, mortgages, real estate, and other real or personal property. We have already pointed out in earlier chapters the tax advantages of corporate vs. individual ownership of passive income-producing property in certain instances (only 30% of corporate stock dividends are taxable, for instance).

Tax Dangers

One aspect of the 1982 federal tax act is especially crucial for personal service corporations. This law permits the IRS to "pierce the corporate veil" in those cases where a corporation performs substantially all of its services for one other corporation, partnership, or other business entity (for example, a corporation of doctors who all work exclusively for one hospital). In such instances, the IRS now has the power to reallocate income and deductions from the professional service corporation to the individual owners (to the financial detriment of the individuals!). The best way to avoid this problem as an incorporated professional is to make sure that your company provides services to more than one client, whether to several hospitals, clinics, or to the public itself. Other devices for assuring the tax-favored status of your professional association can be suggested by a competent legal adviser specializing in this area.

Flat Tax Rate

In the past, professional service corporations enjoyed the same graduated federal corporate tax rates as for-profit corporations. This is no longer the case. Professional service corporations involved in activities or services in the fields of health, law, engineering, architecture, accounting, actuarial science, performing arts, and consulting are now taxed at a flat rate of 34 percent (the lower 15 percent and 25 percent tax brackets are no longer available to these types of corporations). This does not mean that 34 percent of your personal service corporation's income will be paid out to the IRS each year. Only the *profits*, if any, remaining in the corporation at the end of its tax year will be subject to this flat tax rate. Most personal service corporations accumulate little, or no, profits, however, since their income is largely paid out in deductible salaries, retirement plan contributions, and tax-free fringe benefits. Few personal service corporations will consequently pay substantially more taxes as a result of this tax law change. A tax adviser can help you determine if incorporating your practice will result in an increase in tax liability under your individual circumstances.

Personal service corporations, like regular for-profit corporations, have the option of electing to become S corporations and be taxed at personal federal income tax rates, if this proves advantageous. The major disadvantage of S corporations is that certain fringe benefits are not available to them (See Chapter 8, "The S Corporation").

The procedure whereby you can incorporate your practice, virtually the same as for a regular for-profit corporation, will be outlined below. You will want to weigh the advantages and disadvantages of incorporation and seek the advice of a legal counselor concerning the advisability of such a step in your particular case.

INCORPORATING AS A PROFESSIONAL IN MICHIGAN

The Michigan Professional Service Corporation Act authorizes the formation of professional service corporations for the sole purpose of rendering one or more professional services. "Professional service" includes but is not limited to those services rendered by

certified or other public accountants, architects, attorneys, chiropractors, dentists, osteopaths, optometrists, physicians and surgeons, doctors of medicine, doctors of dentistry, podiatrists, chiropodists, professional engineers, veterinarians, and land surveyors.

Other Powers of Professional Service Corporations

In addition to rendering professional services, professional service corporations are also granted the power, under the Michigan Professional Service Corporation Act, to invest their funds in stocks, bonds, real estate, and other forms of investment, as noted above, and to own real or personal property necessary for rendering professional services. How far a professional service corporation may go in making certain types of investments completely unrelated to its professional practices, for example, the purchase of raw land, is unclear under the present law.

Licensing Requirement

The Michigan statutes specify that the shareholders and employees of a professional service corporation must be duly licensed or otherwise legally authorized to render professional service within the state. Of course, clerical and technical employees are exceptions to this rule. Your professional association may employ these types of workers to render services of a non-professional nature.

Limits on Mergers or Consolidations

A professional corporation organized in Michigan can consolidate or merge only with another domestic corporation organized under the Professional Service Corporation Act to render the same professional service or services; a merger or consolidation with any foreign corporation is prohibited.

Annual Report Requirement

There is an annual report requirement for Michigan professional service corporations to assure that non-professionals do not set up and run professional corporations. Each year every professional service corporation must furnish to the Department of Commerce a statement showing the names and addresses of all shareholders of the corporation and shall certify that the corporation meets the requirements of the Professional Service Corporation Act.

Corporate Organization

The manner of organizing a professional service corporation is basically the same as that of a regular for-profit corporation. A minimum of one incorporator is required, who would be the professional practitioner himself or herself. The Articles of Incorporation for professional service corporations is the same form as that for a general business corporation, except that specific mention is made of organization under the Professional Service Corporation Act. A copy of the form is included in Appendix E.

Corporate Name

In completing the Articles, the first item, the corporate name, is subject to the provisions of the general corporation law discussed in Chapter 5. Thus, the name of the professional service corporation must include or end with "Company," "Corporation," "Incorporated," or "Limited," or one of their abbreviated forms ("Co.," "Corp.," "Inc.," or "Ltd."). The name of a corporation organized as a professional service corporation must also contain the words "Professional Corporation" or the abbreviation "P.C."

Specific Purpose Clause Required in Articles

Second, the purpose clause of the Articles must state the particular professional purpose for which the professional association is being organized. A general purpose clause is *not* acceptable. For example, the following formula or a similar one may be used, filling in the name of the particular profession in the blank:

PROFESSIONAL ASSOCIATION: To practice the profession of ____________________, rendering that type of professional service and services ancillary thereto.

Stock Issuance and the Michigan Securities Division

As in the case of a regular for-profit corporation, a professional service corporation issues its stock subject to similar regulations. If you sell stock to more than 10 persons, you will need to contact the Securities Division, since you may be required to register the stock offering and pay a fee.

Professional Corporations Possess the Same Powers and Limitations as Regular Corporations

The powers which regular corporations enjoy and the limitations on regular corporations apply to professional service corporations as well.

Chapter 7. THE MICHIGAN NONPROFIT CORPORATION

Chapter 2108 of the Michigan Nonprofit Corporation Act defines a nonprofit corporation as either: (1) "a corporation formed to carry out any lawful purpose or purposes not involving pecuniary profit or gain for its directors, officers, shareholders, or members (excluding corporations required by law to incorporate under another statute of this state)" *or* (2) "a corporation which has been designated as a tax-exempt organization under section 501(c)(3) of the Internal Revenue Code or is eligible to apply for such a designation." In spite of its nonprofit purpose, employees of a nonprofit corporation are entitled to draw a reasonable salary for services rendered to the corporation, but neither they nor the trustees or members can take earnings out of the corporation in the form of dividends or other personal benefits.

The definitions of nonprofit and charitable corporations in the Michigan statutes are based upon Section 501(c)(3) of the Internal Revenue Code of 1954. A variety of corporations, from those organized to run political campaigns to those engaged in humanitarian endeavors, may be formed under this section.

Nonprofit Articles of Incorporation

A Michigan nonprofit corporation is similar in certain respects to a Michigan profit corporation but different in others. As in the case of a profit corporation, Articles of Incorporation must be filed with the Department of Commerce in order to set up the corporate entity. A copy of the nonprofit Articles is included in Appendix E.

Articles of Incorporation of a nonprofit corporation shall be in the English language (although the name of the corporation need not be in English if written in English letters or Arabic or Roman numerals) and shall set forth:

(1) The name of the corporation.

(2) The purposes for which the corporation is organized. It shall not be sufficient to state substantially that the corporation may engage in any activity within the purposes for which a corporation may be organized under this act (a general purpose clause may *not* be used, as in the case of a corporation organized under the Michigan Business Corporation Act, in other words). A corporation which proposes to conduct educational purposes shall state such purposes and shall comply with all requirements of sections 170 to 177 of Act 327 of the Public Acts of 1931, as amended, being

sections 0450.170 to 450.177 of the Michigan Compiled Acts.

(3) In the case of a corporation organized on a stock basis, the aggregate number of shares which the corporation has authority to issue.

(4) In the case of a corporation organized on a stock basis, if the shares are, or are to be, divided into classes, to the extent that the designations, numbers, relative rights, preferences, and limitations have been determined: the designation of each class; the number of shares in each class; and a statement of the relative rights, preferences, and limitations of the shares of each class.

(5) In the case of a corporation organized on a nonstock basis, a description and statement of the value of any assets of the corporation classified as to real and personal property and the terms of the general scheme of financing the corporation.

(6) In the case of a corporation organized on a nonstock basis, a statement that the corporation is organized on a membership basis or a statement that the corporation is organized on a directorship basis.

(7) The street address, and the mailing address if different from the street address, of the corporation's initial registered office and the name of the corporation's initial resident agent at that address.

(8) The names and addresses of all the incorporators, whether or not fewer than all the incorporators sign the articles, as provided in section 201(2).

(9) The duration of the corporation if other than perpetual.

Names of Nonprofit Corporations

As in the case of profit corporations, the Department of Commerce will not accept any name for a nonprofit corporation which is likely to mislead the public or which indicates or implies that the corporation is organized for a purpose other than one or more of the purposes permitted by its Articles of Incorporation, of if the proposed corporate name is confusingly similar to the name of any other corporation (whether profit or nonprofit, domestic or foreign) or any domestic limited partnership or foreign limited partnership authorized to do business in Michigan. The law provides one exception: a written consent may be filed by the entity with a confusingly similar, but not the same, name, permitting a proposed nonprofit corporation to use such a name. The same procedures for reserving a name, with extensions, or checking the availability of a proposed name by telephone, as discussed in Chapter 5, pages 50-52, may be followed. See the Name Reservation form in Appendix E.

Registered Office and Resident Agent

Like a profit corporation, a nonprofit corporation must also maintain a registered office (which may be the same as its place of business) and a resident agent. This agent may be anyone who is a resident of Michigan, including, but not limited to, one of the incorporators of the corporation. See the discussion of the resident agent's role in Chapter 5. As in the case of a profit corporation, other documents internal to the organization of the corporation, such as the corporate bylaws, are not filed with the Department of Commerce.

Bylaws

After the filing and approval of the Articles by the Department of Commerce, a majority of the incorporators, shareholders, or members of the board may adopt bylaws for the government of the corporation covering such issues as the time and place for holding and the manner of conducting meetings; qualifications for membership and its determination; fees and dues of members; the rights of members; various points concerning the number, qualifications, compensation, and removal of officers; method of changing the bylaws.

Powers of Nonprofit Corporations

The specific authority of nonprofit corporations, which enjoy basically the same powers as profit corporations, is spelled out in Section 450.2261 of the Nonprofit Corporation Act.

See the section on "Powers of Profit Corporations" in Chapter 2 (pages 23-24); nonprofit corporations possess these same powers.

Membership Book, Minutes, Meeting Notices, Officers' Terms, Quorums, Amendments to Articles, and Voluntary Dissolution

The nonprofit corporation is required to keep a membership book with information concerning the name and address of each member, the date of admission to membership, and other pertinent information, in addition to maintaining correct and complete books and records of account, minutes of the proceedings of its incorporators, members (or directors in the case of corporations organized on a directorship basis), and committees. Specific rules paralleling those of profit corporations also govern such matters as how much advance notice members must be given of meetings, officers' terms of office, quorums for meetings, amendments to Articles of Incorporation, and voluntary dissolution.

Major Differences Between Profit and Nonprofit Corporations

The major differences from a profit corporation in the filing of Articles of Incorporation include the following:

(1) A specific nonprofit purpose must be stated in the Articles of a nonprofit corporation.

(2) The name of the corporation does not require a corporate ending, such as inc., corporation, co., and so on.

(3) Nonprofit Articles of Incorporation do not have to be signed by all the incorporators.

(4) The corporation may be organized either on a stock or nonstock basis.

(5) In the latter case, a statement must indicate whether the corporation is to be organized on a membership basis (as in the case of a fraternal organization) or on a directorship basis (as in the case of certain charitable foundations).

(6) Corporations organized on a nonstock basis must also describe and state the value of any assets of the corporation, whether real or personal property, and the proposed scheme of financing the corporation.

(7) The filing fee and franchise fee for a nonprofit Articles of Incorporation is $20.00.

Corporations Involved in the Solicitation of Funds

Any nonprofit corporation (as well as profit corporation) involved in the solicitation of funds for charitable purposes may also need to register with the Charitable Foundation Section of the Office of the Attorney General, 525 W. Ottawa, Room 670, Law Building, Lansing, Michigan 48913 (mailing address: PO Box 30214, Lansing, Michigan 48909); phone (517) 373-1152.

Use of the Name "Foundation"

A corporation incorporated for the purpose of receiving and administering funds for perpetuation of the memory of persons, preservation of objects of historical or natural interest, educational, charitable, or religious purposes, or public welfare may use the name "foundation."

Operation under an Assumed Name

A nonprofit corporation may also operate under an assumed name, by registering the true and assumed names with the Department of Commerce. The appropriate form is available from the Department of Commerce. A $10 fee payment is required to register the fictitious name.

Chapter 8. THE S CORPORATION

An S corporation is a special "small business corporation" which has no more than 35 shareholders. This form of operation is normally adopted by relatively small businesses, but larger firms can also elect S status as long as they meet the limitation on the number of shareholders. The 1981 and 1982 tax acts and the Subchapter S Revision Act of 1982 have made S corporations easier to form and operate. Consequently, the number of such corporations has increased dramatically.

If a business anticipates large start-up losses in the early years of operation, an S selection may be advisable. If, on the other hand, a business has in excess of $185,000 in taxable income *after* salaries, fringe benefits, pension plan contributions and all other expenses have been deducted from gross income, then an S election may also be advantageous. These two situations will be considered in greater depth below. If you plan to elect S status, consultation with an attorney is recommended.

Structure of S Corporations

The S corporation is like a partnership in that it pays no federal taxes in itself.[1] Instead, the income of the corporation is divided in proportion to the stock holdings of the shareholders and is taxed to them as individuals. Likewise, corporate losses are not deducted by the corporation but are passed through directly to the shareholders, who can use the deductions—generally in the year the loss occurs—to offset income from other sources. Like the partnership tax return, the S federal tax return (Form 1120S) is an informational return listing the names of the shareholders and their pro rata share of profits or losses.

Six Requirements for S Status

A corporation can elect S status by the written consent of all the stockholders, provided it meets six requirements:

1. It must be a domestic corporation (i.e., one located anywhere in the United States)

---

[1] The state of Michigan taxes Subchapter S corporations at the same rate as regular corporations. See Chapter 4, under "Michigan Single Business Tax" (page 36).

2. None of the shareholders may be non-resident aliens

3. There must be no more than 35 shareholders (shares held in joint ownership by husband and wife are counted as one shareholder)

4. All shareholders must be individuals or estates or certain trusts (no partnership or corporate shareholders)

5. The corporation can't be a member of a group of affiliated corporations (certain corporations which own stock in other corporations are defined by the IRS as "affiliated")

6. There must be only one class of stock, with all shares having equal rights (differences in regard to voting rights *alone* are permitted, however, allowing for voting and non-voting shares, if desired)

See IRS Publication 589 for more detailed information concerning S election and other special rules governing S corporations.

Advantage of Voting and Non-Voting Stock

In the past, you were barred from adopting S status if your corporation had both voting and non-voting stock. As pointed out in Chapter 2, the Subchapter S Revision Act of 1982 has eliminated this requirement. The creation of non-voting as well as voting stock is now permitted, provided that both voting and non-voting stock are equal in all other respects regarding rights and limitations. This new provision makes it very easy to lower taxes by shifting income to family members in lower tax brackets. By giving non-voting, dividend-paying stock to retired parents or children while keeping voting stock in the hands of the directors of the corporation, you will ease your tax burden without sacrificing control of the company. On the other hand, if your business is profitable and you are receiving all the income yourself (without family members to share it with), a regular corporation will usually give you a lower tax rate than an S corporation, provided taxable income does not exceed roughly $185,000 annually.

Applying to the IRS for S Status

Application for S status is made by completing Form 2553. This form is available from the IRS and must be filed at any time on or before the 15th day of the third month of the corporation's tax year or any time during the preceding tax year. For newly formed corporations which wish to begin as S corporations, this will generally mean filing Form 2553 within 75 days of the date of incorporation. In the event that the IRS later claims non-receipt of the form, it (as well as all other important documents with deadlines) should be sent via certified mail with return receipt requested. This will verify both the mailing and the postmarked date and will stand up in court in the event of any dispute. All the current shareholders of the corporation must agree to the S election, as well as all the persons who were shareholders during the taxable year before the election was made.

Fiscal Year of S Corporations

The fiscal year of newly formed S corporations is now required to be a calendar year (January 1 to December 31) unless there is a business purpose for a fiscal year other than the calendar one.

Revocation of S Status

If stockholders representing a majority of the stock of the corporation file shareholder consents to revocation, S status can be terminated in any successive years. Five years must elapse before you can switch back to S status, however, unless the IRS consents to an earlier re-election. Your S status can also be revoked by the IRS for infringement of the requirements, for instance, if you issue a second class of stock, increase the number of shareholders to more than 35, and so on. Since it may be several years before the IRS discovers that some violation in the past has nullified your S status, a thorough familiarity with the laws governing S corporations is imperative. There are other times when it proves beneficial to a corporation to initiate some action in order deliberately to have its S status revoked.

S Election for Businesses Losing Money

There exist distinct advantages for some individuals in operating an S corporation. If your business is losing money in the first year or two, it may be very beneficial to be able to deduct these losses directly from your personal income on your individual federal income tax return, up to the amount of your basis in the stock of the corporation. In a regular corporation, you have the right to carry these losses forward and deduct them from corporate income in future years when the company is realizing a profit, subject to certain restrictions. Once the S corporation begins to show a profit, earnings will be taxed at individual shareholder, not corporate, rates. At this point, you may choose to terminate the election and revert to a regular corporation or stay as an S, depending on your individual circumstances. As long as the corporation's annual taxable income remains less than $185,000, corporate tax rates will ordinarily prove lower than individual, S corporation rates. Once taxable income begins to exceed $185,000, it is time to explore the possibility of an S election as a tax-saving device.

S Corporation as Family Tax Shelter

As noted above, S corporations work well as "family tax shelters," since business owners with children or other relatives (on friendly terms!) can issue non-voting, dividend-paying stock to these dependents or relations and keep income within the family at lower personal tax rates. For the single owner without dependents, a regular corporation, by contrast, may prove more favorable tax-wise, unless the corporation is very profitable.

S Format for Very Profitable Business

In a very profitable business in which substantial dividends have to be issued to escape the IRS's "accumulated earnings penalty," it may very well be advantageous to avoid double taxation on dividends at both the corporate and individual level by opting for S status and paying out all the earnings of the business each year. With an S corporation, you are more or less required to distribute all the profits of the corporation within two and one-half months of the end of the tax year or suffer severe tax penalties. Profits not so distributed are considered "constructive dividends" by the IRS and taxed to you individually even though they remain in the corporation. Obviously, the S arrangement will not work well for capital-intensive businesses which need to accumulate earnings for large capital expenditures on a regular basis, unless the company is prepared to issue bonds or resort to other similar measures to raise needed capital. Generally speaking, a corporation which can pay out virtually all its earnings each year through a combination of deductible expenses (such as salaries, pension plan contributions, and so on) and dividends will function well as an S. For others, there may be potential problems and tax penalties in the case of undistributed income which is "locked in" the S corporation. This is a complicated area, so plan to consult a tax adviser if you are considering forming an S corporation.

Pension Plans of S Corporations; Fringe Benefits

One previous disadvantage of this form of operation was the much smaller pension plan contributions allowable for S corporations, compared to regular corporations. Many of these differences have now been eliminated. On the minus side, the new law makes previously tax-free medical and life insurance benefits taxable to shareholders who own more than 2 percent of the corporation's stock, beginning in 1987. In other words, there is a trade-off. In exchange for the lower tax rates available to the very profitable S corporation, you lose the opportunity to receive certain tax-free employee fringe benefits.

New Ceiling on Passive Income

The new tax law has made S status attractive for certain groups formerly barred from election, such as investment companies and real estate firms and other businesses which typically have large passive income from interest, dividends, annuities, rents, royalties, and gains from sales or exchanges of stock and securities. In the past, S status was denied to companies whose passive income exceeded 20 percent of gross receipts. Since 1983, the ceiling on passive income has been raised from 20 to 25 percent. Even if a company exceeds this limit, its election will not be terminated if the corporation pays a tax of 46 percent of the passive income in excess of 25 percent of gross receipts. Most importantly, any unincorporated business that becomes an S corporation under the new law or any business that has had S status since it originally incorporated can now receive unlimited passive income.

Pass-Throughs in Like Kind

Another major advantage of the new S corporation is that capital gains and tax-exempt income of the company will be passed through to the shareholders in like kind. That is, it will remain taxable at capital gains rates[2] or be tax-free, as the case may be, whereas in the past all such distributions were treated and taxed as ordinary dividend income to the shareholders.

Other Tax Advantages

Several other tax advantages of the new S corporation center on the treatment of capital gains and net operating losses. Previously, an owner of a company with a net operating loss exceeding the owner's capital investment could not deduct the amount in excess of the owner's "tax basis." This excess amount can now be carried forward and deducted in future years against corporate profits, provided the owner puts additional capital into the corporation equal to the excess loss deducted. Also, shareholders can now report the net operating losses and capital gains of the corpora-

tion separately, whereas in the past the two had to be used to offset each other. For S corporations with capital gains and net operating losses, this can mean a substantial tax savings.

Resolutions to Adopt S Status

After weighing the pros and cons, if you choose to organize your business as an S corporation, resolutions to this effect should be included in the Minutes of the First Meeting of the Board of Directors (see Appendix D). For example,

RESOLVED, that the corporation elect to be treated as a "Small Business Corporation" for income tax purposes under Subchapter S of the Internal Revenue Code.

RESOLVED FURTHER, that the officers of this corporation be and hereby are authorized and directed to obtain the written consent of the shareholders to the foregoing election and to file Form 2553 with the IRS.

These two resolutions to adopt S status have, in fact, already been included in the sample Minutes of the First Meeting of the Board of Directors in Appendix D. If you choose *not* to elect S status, these two resolutions should be crossed out.

---

2   At present, the top capital gains tax rate is 28 percent on long-term gains from assets owned more than 12 months. Only those taxpayers in the highest tax bracket of 31 percent will see a slight difference between the individual federal tax rate and the capital gains rate, therefore. For taxpayers in the lower brackets, the individual rate and the capital gains rate are the same.

APPENDIX A

87

Articles of Incorporation for Profit Corporations

C&S 500 (Rev. 2-92)

MICHIGAN DEPARTMENT OF COMMERCE — CORPORATION AND SECURITIES BUREAU

Date Received

(FOR BUREAU USE ONLY)

Name

Address

City   State   ZIP Code

EFFECTIVE DATE:

DOCUMENT WILL BE RETURNED TO NAME AND ADDRESS INDICATED ABOVE

CORPORATION IDENTIFICATION NUMBER

ARTICLES OF INCORPORATION
For use by Domestic Profit Corporations
(Please read information and instructions on the last page)

Pursuant to the provisions of Act 284, Public Acts of 1972, the undersigned corporation executes the following Articles:

ARTICLE I

The name of the corporation is:

ARTICLE II

The purpose or purposes for which the corporation is formed is to engage in any activity within the purposes for which corporations may be formed under the Business Corporation Act of Michigan.

ARTICLE III

The total authorized shares:

1. Common Shares _______________________________________

   Preferred Shares _______________________________________

2. A statement of all or any of the relative rights, preferences and limitations of the shares of each class is as follows:

ARTICLE IV

1. The address of the registered office is:

____ , Michigan _____________
(Street Address)   (City)   (ZIP Code)

2. The mailing address of the registered office if different from the registered office address:

____ , Michigan _____________
(P.O. Box)   (City)   (ZIP Code)

3. The name of the resident agent at the registered office is: ________________________________

ARTICLE V

The name(s) and address(es) of the incorporator(s) is (are) as follows:

Name   Residence or Business Address

____

____

____

____

____

ARTICLE VI (Optional. Delete if not applicable)

When a compromise or arrangement or a plan of reorganization of this corporation is proposed between this corporation and its creditors or any class of them or between this corporation and its shareholders or any class of them, a court of equity jurisdiction within the state, on application of this corporation or of a creditor or shareholder thereof, or on application of a receiver appointed for the corporation, may order a meeting of the creditors or class of creditors or of the shareholders or class of shareholders to be affected by the proposed compromise or arrangement or reorganization, to be summoned in such manner as the court directs. If a majority in number representing 3/4 in value of the creditors or class of creditors, or of the shareholders or class of shareholders to be affected by the proposed compromise or arrangement or a reorganization, agree to a compromise or arrangement or a reorganization of this corporation as a consequence of the compromise or arrangement, the compromise or arrangement and the reorganization, if sanctioned by the court to which the application has been made, shall be binding on all the creditors or class of creditors, or on all the shareholders or class of shareholders and also on this corporation.

ARTICLE VII (Optional. Delete if not applicable)

Any action required or permitted by the Act to be taken at an annual or special meeting of shareholders may be taken without a meeting, without prior notice, and without a vote, if consents in writing, setting forth the action so taken, are signed by the holders of outstanding shares having not less than the minimum number of votes that would be necessary to authorize or take the action at a meeting at which all shares entitled to vote on the action were present and voted. The written consents shall bear the date of signature of each shareholder who signs the consent. No written consents shall be effective to take the corporate action referred to unless, within 60 days after the record date for determining shareholders entitled to express consent to or to dissent from a proposal without a meeting, written consents signed by a sufficient number of shareholders to take the action are delivered to the corporation. Delivery shall be to the corporation's registered office, its principal place of business, or an officer or agent of the corporation having custody of the minutes of the proceedings of its shareholders. Delivery made to a corporation's registered office shall be by hand or by certified or registered mail, return receipt requested.

Prompt notice of the taking of the corporate action without a meeting by less than unanimous written consent shall be given to shareholders who have not consented in writing.

Use space below for additional Articles or for continuation of previous Articles. Please identify any Article being continued or added. Attach additional pages if needed.

I (We), the incorporator(s) sign my (our) name(s) this __________ day of _______________________________ , 19 _____ .

____   ____

____   ____

____   ____

____   ____

____   ____

Name of person or organization
remitting fees:

____

____

Preparer's name and business
telephone number:

____

( ) _____________________________

INFORMATION AND INSTRUCTIONS

1. The articles of incorporation cannot be filed until this form, or a comparable document, is submitted.

2. Submit one original copy of this document. Upon filing, a microfilm copy will be prepared for the records of the Corporation and Securities Bureau. The original copy will be returned to the address appearing in the box on the front as evidence of filing.

    Since this document must be microfilmed, it is important that the filing be legible. Documents with poor black and white contrast, or otherwise illegible, will be rejected.

3. This document is to be used pursuant to the provisions of Act 284, P.A. of 1972, by one or more persons for the purpose of forming a domestic profit corporation.

4. Article I—The corporate name of a domestic profit corporation is required to contain one of the following words or abbreviations: "Corporation", "Company", "Incorporated", "Limited", "Corp.", "Co.", "Inc.", or "Ltd.".

5. Article II—State, in general terms, the character of the particular business to be carried on. Under section 202(b) of the Act, it is sufficient to state substantially, alone or with specifically enumerated purposes, that the corporation may engage in any activity within the purposes for which corporations may be formed under the Act. The Act requires, however, that educational corporations state their specific purposes.

6. Article IV—A post office box may not be designated as the address of the registered office.

7. Article V—The Act requires one or more incorporators. Educational corporations are required to have three (3) incorporators. The address(es) should include a street number and name (or other designation), city and state.

8. The duration of the corporation should be stated in the articles only if the duration is not perpetual.

9. This document is effective on the date approved and filed by the Bureau. A later effective date, no more than 90 days after the date of delivery, may be stated as an additional article.

10. The articles must be signed in ink by each incorporator. The names of the incorporators as set out in article V should correspond with the signatures.

11. FEES: (Make remittance payable to the State of Michigan). Include corporation name on check or money order.
    Franchise fee: first 60,000 authorized shares or portion thereof... $50.00
        each additional 20,000 authorized shares or portion thereof $30.00
    Non-Refundable filing fee $10.00
    Total minimum fees $60.00

12. Mail form and fee to:
    Michigan Department of Commerce
    Corporation and Securities Bureau
    Corporation Division
    P.O. Box 30054
    6546 Mercantile Way
    Lansing, MI 48909
    Telephone: (517) 334-6302

APPENDIX B

Bylaws

BYLAWS

of

____

ARTICLE I
Location

The principal executive office of the corporation in the State of Michigan shall be located in the City/Village of ___________ and County of ___________. The corporation may have such other offices, either within or without the State of Michigan, as the board of directors may from time to time determine or the business of the corporation may require.

ARTICLE II
Shareholders

<u>Section 1. Place of Meetings.</u> Meetings of the shareholders shall be held at the principal executive office of the corporation or at such other place, within or without the State of Michigan, as the board of directors shall determine.

<u>Section 2. Annual Meeting.</u> The annual meeting of the shareholders shall be held on the ____ day of ___________ at _______A.M./P.M. in each year, for the purpose of electing directors and for the transaction of such additional business as necessary. If the day fixed for the annual meeting shall be a legal holiday, the meeting shall be held on the next succeeding business day at the same hour. If the election of directors shall not be held on the day designated herein for any annual meeting, the board of directors shall cause the election to be held at a meeting of the shareholders as soon thereafter as possible.

<u>Section 3. Special Meetings.</u> Special meetings of the shareholders may be called by the president, by the board of directors, or by the holders of not less than one-fifth of all the outstanding shares of the corporation.

<u>Section 4. Notice of Meetings.</u> Written notice stating the place, date, and hour of meetings shall be delivered not less than ten nor more than sixty days before the date of the meeting, either personally or by mail, by or at the direction of the president, or the secretary, or the officer or persons calling the meeting, to each shareholder of record entitled to vote at such meeting. In the case of a special meeting, the purpose or purposes for which the meeting is called shall be included in the notice. In the case of an annual meeting, those matters which the board at the time of the mailing of the notice intends to present for action by the shareholders (but subject to the provision that any proper matter may be presented at the meeting for such action) shall be set forth. If mailed, the notice is given when deposited in the United States mail, with postage thereon prepaid, directed to the shareholder at his address as it appears on the records of the corporation.

<u>Section 5. Meeting of All Shareholders.</u> If all of the shareholders shall meet at any place and time, either within or without the State of Michigan, and consent to the holding of a meeting at such place and time, such meeting shall be valid without call or notice, and at such meeting any corporate action may be taken.

<u>Section 6. Closing of Transfer Books and Fixing of Record Date.</u> For the purpose of determining shareholders entitled to notice of or to vote at any meeting of the shareholders, or shareholders entitled to receive payment of any dividend, or in order to make a determination of shareholders for any other purpose, the board of directors shall provide that the share transfer books be closed for a stated period but not to exceed, in any case, sixty days. If the share transfer books shall be closed for the purpose of determining shareholders entitled to notice of or to vote at a meeting of shareholders, such books shall be closed for at least ten days, or in the case of a merger or consolidation at least twenty days, immediately preceding such meeting. In lieu of closing the share transfer books, the board of directors may fix in advance a date as the record date for any such determination of shareholders, such date in any case to be not more than sixty days and, for a meeting of shareholders, not less than ten days, or in the case of a merger or consolidation not less than twenty days, immediately preceding the meeting. If a record date is not fixed, (a) the record date for determination of shareholders entitled to notice of or to vote at a meeting of shareholders shall be the close of business on the day next preceding the day on which notice is given, or, if no notice is given, the day next preceding the day on which the meeting is held, and (b) the record date for determining shareholders for any purpose other than that specified in subdivision (a) shall be the close of business on the day on which the resolution of the board relating thereto is adopted.

Section 7. Voting Lists. (1) The officer or agent having charge of the stock transfer books for shares of a corporation shall make and certify a complete list of the shareholders entitled to vote at a shareholders' meeting or any adjournment thereof. The list shall:

(a) Be arranged alphabetically within each class and series, with the address of, and the number of shares held by, each shareholder.

(b) Be produced at the time and place of the meeting.

(c) Be subject to inspection by any shareholder during the whole time of the meeting.

(d) Be *prima facie* evidence as to who are the shareholders entitled to examine the list or to vote at the meeting.

(2) If the requirements of this section have not been complied with, on demand of a shareholder in person or by proxy, who in good faith challenges the existence of sufficient votes to carry any action at the meeting, the meeting shall be adjourned until the requirements are complied with.

Failure to comply with the requirements of this section does not affect the validity of an action taken at the meeting before the making of such a demand.

Section 8. Quorum of Shareholders and Voting by Shareholders. Unless a greater or lesser quorum is provided in the Articles of Incorporation, in a bylaw adopted by the shareholders or in the Michigan Business Corporation Act, shares entitled to case a majority of the votes at a meeting constitute a quorum at the meeting. The shareholders present in person or by proxy at such meeting may continue to do business until adjournment, notwithstanding the withdrawal of enough shareholders to leave less than a quorum. Whether or not a quorum is present, the meeting may be adjourned by a vote of the shares present.

When an action, other than the election of directors, is to be taken by vote of the shareholders, it shall be authorized by a majority of the votes cast by the holders of shares entitled to vote thereon, unless a greater plurality is required by the Articles of Incorporation, or the Michigan Business Corporation Act. Except as otherwise provided by the Articles, directors shall be elected by a plurality of votes cast at an election.

Section 9. Voting of Shares. Subject to the provisions of Section 12 of this Article, each outstanding share, regardless of class, shall be entitled to one vote upon each matter submitted at a meeting of shareholders, unless the Articles of Incorporation provide otherwise.

Section 10. Proxies. At all meetings of shareholders, a shareholder may vote either in person or by proxy executed in writing by the shareholder or by his duly authorized agent or representative. No proxy shall be valid after 3 years from the date of its execution, unless otherwise provided in the proxy.

Section 11. Voting of Shares by Certain Holders. Shares standing in the name of another corporation—domestic or foreign—may be voted by such officer, agent, or proxy as the Bylaws of such corporation may prescribe, or, in the absence of such provision, as the board of directors of such corporation may determine.

Shares of its own stock belonging to this corporation shall not be voted, directly or indirectly, at any meeting and shall not be counted in determining the total number of outstanding shares entitled to vote at any given time, but shares of its own stock held by it in a fiduciary capacity may be voted and shall be counted in determining the total number of outstanding shares entitled to vote at any given time.

Shares standing in the name of a receiver may be voted by such receiver, and shares held by or under the control of a receiver may be voted by such receiver without the transfer thereof into his name if authority so to do is contained in an appropriate order of the court by which such receiver was appointed.

Shares standing in the name of a deceased person, a minor ward or an incompetent person, may be voted by his administrator, executor, court-appointed guardian or conservator, either in person or by proxy without a transfer of shares into the name of such administrator, executor, court-appointed guardian or conservator. Shares standing in the name of a trustee may be voted by him, either in person or by proxy.

A shareholder whose shares are pledged shall be entitled to vote such shares until the shares have been transferred into the name of the pledgee, and thereafter the pledgee shall be entitled to vote the shares so transferred.

Section 12. Cumulative Voting. The Articles of Incorporation may provide that every shareholder in all elections for directors shall exercise cumulative voting rights. In so doing, each shareholder shall have the right to vote, in person or by proxy, the number of shares owned by him, for as many persons as there are directors to be elected, or to cumulate said shares, and give one candidate as many votes as the number of directors multiplied by the number of his shares shall equal, or to distribute them on the same principle among as many candidates as he shall think fit.

Section 13. Inspectors. At any meeting of shareholders, the chairman of the meeting may, or upon the request of any shareholder shall, appoint one or more persons as inspectors for such meeting.

Such inspectors shall ascertain and report the number of shares represented at the meeting, the existence of a quorum, and the validity and effect of proxies; count all votes and report the results; and do such other acts as are proper to conduct the election and voting with impartiality and fairness to all the shareholders.

Each report of an inspector shall be in writing and signed by him or by a majority of them if there be more than one inspector acting at such meeting. If there is more than one inspector, the report of a majority shall be the report of the inspectors. The report of the inspector or inspectors on the number of shares represented at the meeting and the results of the voting shall be *prima facie* evidence thereof.

Section 14. Action without Meeting. Any action which may be taken at any annual or special meeting of shareholders may be taken without a meeting, without prior notice, and without a vote, setting forth the action so taken, by means of written consents signed by the holders of all the outstanding shares entitled to vote or signed by such lesser number of holders as may be provided for in the Articles of Incorporation, but not less than the minimum number of votes that would be necessary to authorize or take the action at a meeting at which all shares entitled to vote thereon were present and voted. The written consents shall bear the date of signature of each shareholder who signs the consent.

ARTICLE III
Directors

Section 1. Powers. Subject to any provision in the Articles of Incorporation, the business and affairs of the corporation shall be managed by a board of directors.

Section 2. Number. The authorized number of directors shall be _____ until changed by amendment to this Article of these Bylaws.

Section 3. Election and Term of Directors. Each director shall hold office until the next annual meeting of shareholders or until his successor shall have been elected and qualified, or until his prior resignation or removal. Unless otherwise provided in the Articles of Incorporation, a director may be removed, with or without cause, by vote of the holders of a majority of the shares entitled to vote at an election of directors. Directors need not be residents of Michigan or shareholders of the corporation.

Section 4. Vacancies. Any vacancy occurring in the board of directors and any directorship to be filled by reason of an increase in the number of directors may be filled by election at an annual meeting or at a special meeting of shareholders called for that purpose; however, if authorized by the Articles of Incorporation or an amendment thereto a majority of directors then in office may properly fill one or more vacancies arising between meetings of shareholders by reason of an increase in the number of directors or otherwise, but at no time may the number of directors selected to fill vacancies in this manner during the interim period between meetings of shareholders exceed 33 1/3% of the total membership of the board of directors. A director elected to fill a vacancy shall serve until the next annual meeting of shareholders.

Section 5. Regular Meetings. A regular meeting of the board of directors shall be held without other notice than this Bylaw, immediately after and at the same place as the annual meeting of shareholders. The board of directors may provide, by resolution, the time and place, for the holding of additional regular meetings without other notice than this resolution.

Section 6. Manner of Convening Special Meetings. Special meetings of the board of directors may be called by or at the request of the president or any two directors.

Section 7. Place of Special Meetings. The person or persons authorized to convene special meetings of the board of directors may fix any place, either within or without the State of Michigan, as the place for holding any special meeting of the board of directors.

Section 8. Notice of Directors' Meetings. Special meetings of the board of directors shall be held upon at least four days' prior notice in writing, delivered personally or mailed to the business address of each director. Any director may waive notice of any meeting. Attendance of a director at any meeting shall constitute a waiver of notice of such meeting except where a director attends a meeting for the express purpose of objecting to the transaction of any business because the meeting is not lawfully called or convened. Neither the business to be transacted at not the purpose of any regular or special meeting of the board of directors need be specified in the notice or waiver of notice of such meeting.

Section 9. Quorum of Directors. A majority of the number of directors fixed by the Bylaws shall constitute a quorum for the transaction of business. The act of the majority of the directors present at a meeting at which a quorum is present shall be the act of the board of directors.

Section 10. Informal Action by Directors. Unless specifically prohibited by the Articles of Incorporation, any action required to be taken at a meeting of the board of directors may be taken without a meeting if a consent in writing, setting forth the action so taken, shall be signed by all the directors entitled to vote.

<u>Section 11. Dissent.</u> A director of a corporation who is present at a meeting of its board of directors at which action on any corporate matter is taken is conclusively presumed to have assented to the action taken unless his dissent is entered into the minutes of the meeting or unless he files his written dissent to such action with the person acting as the secretary of the meeting before the adjournment thereof or forwards such dissent by registered mail to the secretary of the corporation immediately after the adjournment of the meeting. Such right to dissent does not apply to a director who voted in favor of such action.

<u>Section 12. Compensation.</u> By the affirmative vote of a majority of directors, the board shall have authority to establish reasonable compensation for directors in payment for actual services to the corporation. A fixed sum and expenses for actual attendance at each regular or special meeting of the board may also be authorized.

ARTICLE IV
Officers

<u>Section 1. Number.</u> The officers of the corporation shall be a president, a vice-president, a secretary and a treasurer, as well as other additional officers whose titles and duties shall be determined by the board of directors. Any two or more offices may be held by the same person, but an officer shall not execute, acknowledge, or verify an instrument in more than one capacity if the instrument is required by law or the Articles of Incorporation to be executed, acknowledged, or verified by 2 or more officers.

<u>Section 2. Election.</u> An officer of the corporation shall be chosen by the board of directors. Each officer shall hold office until his death, resignation or removal as hereinafter provided. A vacancy in any office because of death, resignation or removal or other cause shall be filled by the board at either an annual or special meeting.

<u>Section 3. Resignation and Removal.</u> An officer may resign at any time upon written notice to the corporation. An officer may be removed at any time, either with or without cause, by the board, but such removal shall be without prejudice to the contract rights, if any, of the person so removed.

<u>Section 4. President.</u> The president shall be the chief executive officer of the corporation, and, subject to the direction and control of the board of directors, shall manage the business of the corporation and shall see that all orders and resolutions of the board are carried out. He or she shall preside at all meetings of the shareholders and directors and shall have such other powers and duties as may from time to time be prescribed by the board of directors or Bylaws.

<u>Section 5. Vice-President.</u> During the absence or disability of the president, the vice-president, or, if there are more than one, the executive vice-president, shall possess all powers and functions of the president. Any vice-president may sign, with the secretary, certificates for shares of the corporation, and shall perform such other duties as may from time to time be prescribed by the board of directors or the Bylaws.

<u>Section 6. Secretary.</u> The secretary shall keep or cause to be kept, at the principal executive office of the corporation, the minutes of all meetings of the shareholders and of the board of directors. The secretary shall see that all notices of meetings are given in accordance with the provisions of these Bylaws or as required by law. The secretary shall have charge of the corporate seal and shall affix it to any instrument when authorized by the board of directors. The secretary shall keep or cause to be kept, at the principal executive office of the corporation or at the office of the corporation's transfer agent, a share register, showing the names of the shareholders and their addresses, the number and classes of shares held by each, the number and date of certificates issued for shares, and the number and date of cancellation of every certificate surrendered for cancellation. The secretary shall keep or cause to be kept, at the principal executive office of the corporation, the original or a copy of the Bylaws and amendments, and shall perform whatever other duties as may be prescribed by the board.

<u>Section 7. Treasurer.</u> The treasurer shall have charge of the corporate funds and securities; shall keep or cause to be kept complete and accurate account books of corporate receipts and payments; deposit all money and other valuables in the name of the corporation in such banks, trust companies or other depositories as designated by the board of directors; prepare and present financial reports to the annual meeting of shareholders and the regular meetings of the board of directors, and perform such other duties as are assigned to him or her from time to time by the board of directors.

<u>Section 8. Sureties and Bonds.</u> If required by the board of directors, any officer of the corporation shall give to the corporation a bond for the faithful performance of his duties in such sum and with such surety or sureties as the board shall determine.

<u>Section 9. Compensation.</u> The salaries of the officers shall be fixed from time to time by the board of directors. No officer shall be prevented from receiving such salary due to the fact that he is also a director of the corporation.

ARTICLE V
Certificates for Shares

<u>Section 1. Certificates.</u> The shares of the corporation shall be represented by certificates. The form of such certificates shall be determined by the board of directors, in accordance with the requirements of the Michigan Business Corporation Act. All certificates shall be numbered and entered in the books of the corporation upon issue. They shall show the holder's name and the number of shares and shall be signed by the president or a vice-president and by the secretary and shall bear the corporate seal. In addition, they shall state that the corporation is formed under the laws of the state of Michigan and shall indicate (1) the class of shares (if there is more than one), (2) the designation of the series (if any), and (3) the par value of each share represented by the certificate, or a statement that the shares are without par value. In the case of a lost or destroyed certificate, an affidavit of the fact shall be made by the person claiming the certificate to be lost or destroyed. The board may direct a new certificate to be issued as a replacement for that one alleged to be lost or stolen and may, at its discretion, require a bond as indemnity against any claims that may arise regarding the certificate alleged lost or stolen.

<u>Section 2. Transfer of Shares.</u> All certificates surrendered to the corporation by the holder of record or his authorized representative shall be cancelled and a new certificate issued to the transferee. All such transfers shall be entered in the transfer book of the corporation, kept at its principal executive office or the office of its transfer agent. No transfer shall be made within ten days preceding the annual meeting of shareholders. The holder of record of any share shall be regarded as the holder in fact for all purposes as regards the corporation.

ARTICLE VI
Waiver of Notice

Any notice required to be given under the provisions of these Bylaws, the Articles of Incorporation, or the provisions of The Business Corporation Act may be waived by the individual entitled to such notice. A waiver in writing signed by said individual, whether before or after the time stated in the notice, shall be deemed equivalent to the giving of such notice.

ARTICLE VII
Dividends

The board of directors may declare and the corporation may pay dividends on its outstanding shares from time to time, subject to the provisions of The Business Corporation Act and the corporation's Articles of Incorporation: No dividends shall be declared or paid at a time when the corporation is insolvent or its net assets are less than its stated capital, or when the payment thereof would render the corporation insolvent or reduce its net assets below its stated capital. Dividends may be declared or paid and other distributions may be made out of surplus only.

ARTICLE VIII
Amendment of Bylaws

Bylaws may be adopted, altered, amended, or repealed at any meeting of the board of directors of the corporation by a majority vote of the directors present at the meeting.

CERTIFICATE

This is to certify that the foregoing is a true and correct copy of the Bylaws of the corporation named in the title thereto and that such Bylaws were duly adopted by the board of directors of said corporation on the date set forth below.

DATED:

____
Secretary

(seal)

APPENDIX C

**Waiver of Notice
Minutes of First Meeting of Shareholders**

WAIVER OF NOTICE AND CONSENT TO HOLDING OF FIRST MEETING OF SHAREHOLDERS

of

____

We, the undersigned, being all the shareholders of _________________, a Michigan corporation, hereby waive notice of the first meeting of the shareholders of the Corporation and consent to the holding of said meeting at _________________ in _____________________, Michigan, on ____________, 19 ____, at ________A.M./P.M., and consent to the transaction of any and all business by the Shareholders at the meeting, including, without limitation, the approval of the Articles of Incorporation, the recording of the Certificate of Incorporation, the approval of the preorganization subscription agreement (if applicable), and the election of directors.

DATED:

____
Shareholder

____
Shareholder

____
Shareholder

____
Shareholder

____
Shareholder

____
Shareholder

MINUTES OF FIRST MEETING OF SHAREHOLDERS
OF

____

The Shareholders of _______________________________________ held its first meeting on
____________________, 19 _____ at _________ A.M./P.M. at _________________________________ in
__________________, Michigan. Written waiver of notice was signed by all the Shareholders and attached
to the minutes of this meeting.

      The following Shareholders, being the owners of a majority of the outstanding shares and
constituting a quorum, were present at the meeting:

             ____

             ____

             ____

             ____

             ____

             ____

These were represented by proxy:

             ____

             ____

             ____

These were absent:

             ____

             ____

             ____

      On motion and by unanimous vote, ______________________________ was elected temporary
Chairman and presided over the meeting. ______________________________ was elected temporary Secretary
of the meeting.

      The Chairman advised that the Articles of Incorporation had been filed and a Certificate of
Incorporation issued by the Michigan Department of Commerce. Upon the presentation of these documents to the
meeting, a motion was duly made, seconded and unanimously carried that the Articles of Incorporation be approved
and the Certificate recorded.

      The Chairman presented to the meeting the preorganization subscription agreement (if applicable)
of the Corporation. It was read and formally approved by the Shareholders.

      By unanimous vote, the following persons were elected Directors, to hold office until the next
annual meeting of Shareholders, and until the election and qualification of their successors:

NAME   ADDRESS

_______________________   _______________________

_______________________   _______________________

_______________________   _______________________

_______________________   _______________________

_______________________   _______________________

      Since there was no further business to come before the meeting, on motion duly made and seconded,
the meeting was adjourned.

DATED:

____
Secretary

The following are appended hereto:
      WAIVER OF NOTICE OF MEETING
      COPY OF CERTIFICATE OF INCORPORATION
      PREORGANIZATION SUBSCRIPTION AGREEMENT (if applicable)

APPENDIX D

**Waiver of Notice
Minutes of First Meeting of Board of Directors**

WAIVER OF NOTICE AND CONSENT TO HOLDING OF FIRST MEETING OF BOARD OF DIRECTORS
OF
____

We, the undersigned, being all the directors of _______________________, a Michigan corporation, hereby waive notice of the first meeting of the board of directors of the corporation and consent to the holding of said meeting at _____________________ in _____________________, Michigan, on ________________, 19 _____, at _______A.M./P.M., and consent to the transaction of any and all business by the directors at the meeting, including, without limitation, the adoption of Bylaws, the election of officers, the adoption of the corporate seal and stock certificates, the establishment of the corporation's fiscal year, and the selection of a bank or banks where the corporation will maintain accounts.

DATED:

____
Director

____
Director

____
Director

____
Director

MINUTES OF FIRST MEETING OF BOARD OF DIRECTORS
OF

____

The first meeting of the board of directors was held at _________________
_____________ in _______________________, Michigan, on _____________, 19_____, at ______ A.M./P.M.
The following directors, constituting a quorum of all the directors of the corporation, were present.

____

____

____

____

_______________________________ was nominated and by unanimous vote elected temporary chairman, and presided over the meeting until relieved by the president.
_______________________________ was nominated and elected by unanimous vote as temporary secretary, and acted as such until relieved by the permanent secretary. The secretary then presented to the meeting the Waiver of Notice of Meeting signed by all the directors, and upon a motion duly made, seconded, and carried, the waiver was appended to the minutes of the meeting.

The chairman then presented to the meeting a certified copy of the Articles of Incorporation which had been filed with the Michigan Department of Commerce on _______________________, 19 _____. The secretary was instructed to append the copy to the minutes of the meeting.

The chairman thereupon presented to the meeting a copy of the proposed bylaws of the corporation. After consideration and discussion, it was unanimously

RESOLVED, that the corporation adopt as the bylaws of this corporation the bylaws presented to this meeting.

The following persons were nominated and unanimously elected officers of the corporation to serve for one year and until their successors are elected and qualified:
_______________________________ President
_______________________________ Vice-President
_______________________________ Secretary
_______________________________ Treasurer

The president thereafter presided at the meeting and the permanent secretary replaced the temporary secretary.

Upon motion duly made, seconded, and carried, it was

RESOLVED, that the form of the corporate seal presented at the meeting, an impression of which is directed to be made by the secretary in the margin of these minutes, be and hereby is adopted as the seal of this corporation.

Upon motion duly made, seconded, and carried, it was further

RESOLVED, that the form of stock certificate submitted to this meeting be and hereby is adopted for the issuance of share certificates by the president and secretary. A copy of the stock certificate so adopted is to be attached to these minutes, and further

RESOLVED, that the principal executive office of this corporation shall be at
_______________________________ in _______________________, Michigan.
Upon motion duly made, seconded, and carried, it was

RESOLVED, that the fiscal year of this corporation shall end on the _____ day of the month of _______________________ of each year.
Upon motion duly made, seconded, and carried, it was

RESOLVED, that the treasurer be and hereby is authorized to open a bank account with
_______________________________ located at _______________________________________ and a resolution for that purpose on the printed form of said bank(s) was adopted and instructed to be attached to these minutes.

Upon motion duly made, seconded,and carried, it was

RESOLVED, that the Medical Reimbursement Plan presented to this meeting be and hereby is adopted as the medical reimbursement plan of the corporation.

Upon motion duly made, seconded, and carried, it was

RESOLVED, that the following annual salaries be paid to the officers of this corporation:
PRESIDENT;
VICE-PRESIDENT:
SECRETARY:
TREASURER:

Upon motion duly made, seconded, and carried, it was

RESOLVED, that the corporation elect to be treated as a "Small Business Corporation" for income tax purposes under Subchapter S of the Internal Revenue Code.

RESOLVED FURTHER, that the officers of this corporation be and hereby are authorized and directed to obtain the written consent of the shareholders to the foregoing election and to file Form 2553 with the IRS.

RESOLVED, that the officers of the corporation be authorized to sell and issue shares of stock in exchange for money and property, not to exceed $1,000,000 in amount, and further

RESOLVED, that this sale and the organizing and managing of the corporation shall be carried out as a "Small Business Corporation," to the end that any shareholder who experiences a loss on the transfer of shares of common stock of the corporation may qualify for an "ordinary" loss deduction on his personal income tax return.

Upon motion duly made, seconded, and carried, it was

RESOLVED, that whereas the Articles of Incorporation authorize the issuance of _________________ shares of capital stock, this corporation shall sell an aggregate of not to exceed ________ shares of its capital stock at a purchase price of $_____ per share, in consideration of money paid to the corporation, as follows:

Name(s) of Purchaser(s)   Number of Shares   Amount of Money

RESOLVED FURTHER, that this corporation sell and issue an aggregate of not to exceed _______ shares of its capital stock at a purchase price of $_______ per share, upon delivery of said assets to the corporation, as follows:

Name(s) of Purchaser(s)   Number of Shares   Description of Property

Upon motion duly made, seconded, and carried, it was

RESOLVED, that the corporation accept the written offer dated ___________________________, 19 _____, to transfer the assets and liabilities of said business, in accordance with the terms of said offer, a copy of which is attached to the minutes of this meeting.

RESOLVED FURTHER, that the board of directors hereby determine that the fair market value of said business to the corporation is $____________.

Since there was no further business to come before the meeting, on motion duly made, seconded, and carried, the meeting was adjourned.

DATED:

____
Secretary

The following are appended hereto:
WAIVER OF NOTICE OF MEETING
CERTIFIED COPY OF ARTICLES OF INCORPORATION
SAMPLE STOCK CERTIFICATE
BANK DEPOSITORY RESOLUTION FORM
MEDICAL REIMBURSEMENT PLAN (if applicable)
OFFER OF TRANSFER OF BUSINESS (if applicable)

APPENDIX E

Name Reservation Application
Preorganization Subscription Agreement
Articles of Incorporation for Professional Service
Corporations
Incorporation under a Close Corporation Agreement
Bill of Sale Agreement
Medical and Dental Reimbursement Plan
Articles of Incorporation for Nonprofit Corporations

CS 540 Rev. 1.91

(FOR BUREAU USE ONLY)

Date Received

EXPIRATION DATE:

APPLICATION FOR RESERVATION OF NAME
For use by Corporations and Limited Partnerships
(Please read information and instructions on reverse side)

Pursuant to the provisions of Act 284, Public Acts of 1972 (profit corporations), Act 162, Public Acts of 1982 (nonprofit corporations), or Act 213, Public Acts of 1982, (limited partnerships), the undersigned applicant executes the following Application:

1. The name to be reserved is:

2. This name is to be used for a: (check one)

□ Michigan profit corporation

□ Foreign profit corporation

□ Michigan nonprofit corporation

□ Foreign nonprofit corporation

□ Michigan limited partnership

□ Foreign limited partnership

Signed this _______ day of _______________________ , 19 ____

____
(Signature)

_________________________________   _______________
(Type or Print Name)   (Type or Print Title)

____
(Street Address)

____
(City, State, ZIP Code)

NOTICE OF TRANSFER OF NAME RESERVATION

This notice of transfer will be required in the event that corporate or limited partnership documents are submitted under the reserved name by someone other than the person reserving the name.

Pursuant to the provisions of Section 215(3), Act 284, Public Acts of 1972, or Section 215(3), Act 162, Public Acts of 1982, or Section 103(b) of Act 213, Public Acts of 1982, the undersigned hereby transfers to

____

____
(Name and Address of Transferee)

the right to exclusive use of the name ____

____ for business purposes in the State of

Michigan.

____
(Name of Original Applicant)

By ____
(Signature)

INFORMATION AND INSTRUCTIONS

1. Submit one original copy of this Application, or a comparable document, to apply for a name reservation. After filing, a true copy will be returned by the Bureau to the person submitting the document.

2. If the name is available, the administrator shall reserve it for exclusive use of the applicant for a period expiring at the end of the fourth full calendar month following the month in which the application was filed. The administrator, for good cause shown, may extend the reservation for periods of not more than two calendar months each. No more than two extensions shall be granted. Extension requests must be received by the Bureau prior to the expiration of the reservation period. The exclusive right to use a name may be transferred to another person by the applicant for whom the name was reserved, by executing and filing a notice of transfer and stating the name of the transferee.

3. The application for reservation of name and the notice of transfer of name reservation must be signed in ink by the applicant.

4. FEES: (Make remittance payable to State of Michigan)..$10.00
No fee for transfer or extension of reservation.

5. Mail form and fee to:

Michigan Department of Commerce
Corporation and Securities Bureau
Corporation Division
PO Box 30054
6546 Mercantile Way
Lansing, MI 48909
Telephone (517) 334-6302

PREORGANIZATION SUBSCRIPTION AGREEMENT

We, the undersigned, severally subscribe to the number of shares set opposite our respective names of capital stock of a proposed corporation, to be known as ____ or by any other name that the incorporators may select, and to be incorporated in the State of Michigan. We agree to pay the sum of $_______ per each share subscribed.

This subscription shall not be binding on the undersigned unless subscriptions in the aggregate amount of $___________ for shares of said corporation have been procured on or before the _____ day of __________________________, 19 ______.

All subscriptions hereto shall be payable at such time or times as the board of directors of said corporation may determine and shall be paid in cash, except as hereinafter indicated. (If any of the subscriptions are to be paid by transferring property to the corporation, a description of the property shall be attached hereto.)

Date	Name and Address	Number of Shares	Amount Subscribed

&S 501 (Rev. 6-92)

MICHIGAN DEPARTMENT OF COMMERCE — CORPORATION AND SECURITIES BUREAU

Date Received			**(FOR BUREAU USE ONLY)**

Name

Address

City　　　　　　State　　　　　　ZIP Code

EFFECTIVE DATE:

DOCUMENT WILL BE RETURNED TO NAME AND ADDRESS INDICATED ABOVE

CORPORATION IDENTIFICATION NUMBER

ARTICLES OF INCORPORATION

For use by Domestic Profit Professional Service Corporations

(Please read instructions and Paperwork Reduction Act notice on last page)

Pursuant to the provisions of Act 192, Public Acts of 1962, as amended, the undersigned corporation executes the following Articles:

ARTICLE I

The name of the corporation is:

ARTICLE II

This corporation is organized for the sole and specific purpose of rendering the following professional service(s):

ARTICLE III

The total authorized shares:

1. Common Shares ____

    Preferred Shares ____

2. A statement of all or any of the relative rights, preferences and limitations of the shares of each class is as follows:

ARTICLE IV

1. The address of the registered office is:

____ , Michigan _____________
(Street Address)   (City)   (ZIP Code)

2. The mailing address of the registered office if different than above:

____ , Michigan _____________
(P.O. Box)   (City)   (ZIP Code)

3. The name of the resident agent at the registered office is: _________________________

ARTICLE V

The name(s) and address(es) of the incorporator(s) is (are) as follows:

Name   Residence or Business Address

____

____

____

____

____

ARTICLE VI (Optional. Delete if not applicable)

When a compromise or arrangement or a plan of reorganization of this corporation is proposed between this corporation and its creditors or any class of them or between this corporation and its shareholders or any class of them, a court of equity jurisdiction within the state, on application of this corporation or of a creditor or shareholder thereof, or on application of a receiver appointed for the corporation, may order a meeting of the creditors or class of creditors or of the shareholders or class of shareholders to be affected by the proposed compromise or arrangement or reorganization, to be summoned in such manner as the court directs. If a majority in number representing 3/4 in value of the creditors or class of creditors, or of the shareholders or class of shareholders to be affected by the proposed compromise or arrangement or a reorganization, agree to a compromise or arrangement or a reorganization of this corporation as a consequence of the compromise or arrangement, the compromise or arrangement and the reorganization, if sanctioned by the court to which the application has been made, shall be binding on all the creditors or class of creditors, or on all the shareholders or class of shareholders and also on this corporation.

ARTICLE VII (Optional. Delete if not applicable)

Any action required or permitted by the Act to be taken at an annual or special meeting of shareholders may be taken without a meeting, without prior notice, and without a vote, if consents in writing, setting forth the action so taken, are signed by the holders of outstanding shares having not less than the minimum number of votes that would be necessary to authorize or take the action at a meeting at which all shares entitled to vote on the action were present and voted. The written consents shall bear the date of signature of each shareholder who signs the consent. No written consents shall be effective to take the corporate action referred to unless, within 60 days after the record date for determining shareholders entitled to express consent to or to dissent from a proposal without a meeting, written consents signed by a sufficient number of shareholders to take the action are delivered to the corporation. Delivery shall be to the corporation's registered office, its principal place of business, or an officer or agent of the corporation having custody of the minutes of the proceedings of its shareholders. Delivery made to a corporation's registered office shall be by hand or by certified or registered mail, return receipt requested.

Prompt notice of the taking of the corporate action without a meeting by less than unanimous written consent shall be given to shareholders who have not consented in writing.

Use space below for additional Articles or for continuation of previous Articles. Please identify any Article being continued or added. Attach additional pages if needed.

(we), the incorporator(s) sign my (our) name(s) this __________ day of ___________________________ , 19 _____ .

_________________________________   _________________________________

_________________________________   _________________________________

_________________________________   _________________________________

_________________________________   _________________________________

_________________________________   _________________________________

Name of person or organization
remitting fees:

____

____

Preparer's name and business
telephone number:

____

(   ) ________________________

INFORMATION AND INSTRUCTIONS

1. This form is issued under the authority of Act 192, P.A. of 1962, as amended. The articles of incorporation cannot be filed until this form, or a comparable document, is submitted.

2. Submit one original copy of this document. Upon filing, a microfilm copy will be prepared for the records of the Corporation and Securities Bureau. The original copy will be returned to the address appearing in the box on the front as evidence of filing.

   Since this document must be microfilmed, it is important that the filing be legible. Documents with poor black and white contrast, or otherwise illegible, will be rejected.

3. This document is to be used pursuant to the provisions of Act 192, P.A. of 1962 by one or more persons for the purpose of forming a domestic profit professional service corporation.

4. Article I—The corporate name shall contain the words "Professional Corporation" or the abbreviation "P.C."

5. Article II—State the specific professional service(s) for which the corporation is organized.

6. Article III—Indicate the total number of shares which the corporation has authority to issue. If there is more than one class or series of shares, state the relative rights, preferences and limitations of the shares of each class in Article III(2).

7. Article IV—A post office box may not be designated as the street address of the registered office.

8. Article V—The Act requires one or more incorporator(s) who, except as otherwise provided or prohibited, must be licensed to perform at least one of the service(s) for which the corporation is organized. The address(es) should include a street number and name (or other designation), city and state.

9. If the professional corporation renders a professional service that is included within the public health code, Act No. 368 of the Public Acts of 1978, being sections 333.1101 to 333.25211 of the Michigan Compiled Laws, then all shareholders of the corporation shall be licensed or legally authorized in this state to render the same professional service, as provided for in Public Act 166 of 1990.

10. The duration of the corporation should be stated in the articles only if the duration is not perpetual.

11. This document is effective on the date endorsed "Filed" by the Bureau. A later effective date, no more than 90 days after the date of delivery, may be stated as an additional article.

12. The articles must be signed in ink by each incorporator. The names of the incorporators as set out in article V should correspond with the signatures.

13. FEES: (Make remittance payable to the State of Michigan. Include corporation name on check or money order)

    Franchise fee: first 60,000 authorized shares or portion thereof $50.00
    each additional 20,000 authorized shares or portion thereof $30.00
    Non-Refundable filing fee $10.00
    TOTAL MINIMUM FEES $60.00

12. Mail form and fee to:

Michigan Department of Commerce	The office is located at:
Corporation and Securities Bureau	6546 Mercantile Way
Corporation Division	Lansing, MI 48910
P.O. Box 30054	
Lansing, Michigan 48909	
Telephone: (517) 334-6302	

INCORPORATION UNDER A CLOSE CORPORATION AGREEMENT

The Articles of Incorporation must list one or more restrictions on the transfer of issued shares of stock under Article III, item 3, or in the section provided for additional Articles. Such restrictions must be uniform within each class. The stock certificates of your close corporation must spell out the restriction(s).

The following types of restrictions may be listed in your Articles of Incorporation:

RIGHT OF FIRST REFUSAL. This kind of restriction requires a shareholder to offer to the corporation or to one or more shareholders of the corporation or to any other designated person or to any combination of the above a prior opportunity to acquire his or her shares.

PRIOR CONSENT. This kind of restriction obligates the corporation or the holders of shares of any class of the corporation to consent to any proposed transferee of the shares.

SUBCHAPTER S TRANSFERS. This type of restriction prohibits a transfer of shares if such would cause the corporation to lose its elected status as a "small business corporation" under Subchapter S of the Internal Revenue Code.

PROHIBITED TRANSFERS. This type of restriction forbids a transfer of shares to designated persons or classes of persons, provided such a prohibition is not manifestly unreasonable.

OTHERS. Any other lawful restriction on transfer of shares may be made in the Articles of Incorporation.

BILL OF SALE AGREEMENT

The corporation, _________________________________, and the business owner(s)
_________________________________, hereafter called the "transferor(s)," enter into the following
agreement:

     1. In return for the issuance and delivery of _______ shares of stock of ______________
_____________, a Michigan corporation, I (we) hereby sell, assign, and transfer to the corporation all my (our) right,
title, and interest in the following property:

     a. All the tangible assets listed on the inventory attached to this Bill of Sale, and all stock in trade,
trade, goodwill, trade names, trademarks, service marks, leasehold interests, copyrights and other intangible assets
(excluding—list any non-transferred assets) of ____, located at
_________________________________ Street, ______________________________,
_________________ County, Michigan.

     2. In return for the transfer of the above property to it, the corporation hereby agrees to assume, pay,
and discharge all debts, duties, and obligations that appear on the date of this agreement, on the books and owed on
account of said business (excluding—list any unassumed liabilities). The corporation agrees to indemnify and hold
the transferor(s) of said business and their property free from any liability for any such debt, duty, or obligation and
from any suits, actions, or legal proceedings brought to enforce or collect any such debt, duty, or obligation.

     3. The transferor(s) hereby appoint(s) the corporation as his (her, their) representative to demand,
receive, and collect for itself, all debts and obligations now owing to said business (excluding—list any unassumed
debts). The transferor(s) further authorize(s) the corporation to do all things allowed by law to recover and collect
such debts and obligations and to use the transferor's (s') name(s) in such manner as it considers necessary for the
collection and recovery of such debts and obligations, provided, however, without cost, expense, or damage to the
transferor(s).

DATED:

____
(Transferor)

____
(Transferor)

____
(Transferor)

____
(Name of Corporation)
By: _________________________________
     (Title)

____
     (Title)

MEDICAL AND DENTAL CARE REIMBURSEMENT PLAN
OF

____

1. BENEFITS

The corporation shall reimburse all eligible employees for expenses incurred by themselves and their dependents, as defined in IRC S152, as amended, for medical care, as defined in IRC S213(e), as amended, subject to the conditions and limitations as hereinafter set forth. It is the intention of the Corporation that the benefits payable to eligible employees hereunder shall be excluded from their gross income pursuant to IRC S105, as amended.

2. ELIGIBILITY.

All corporate officers employed on a full-time basis at the date of inception of this Plan, including those who may be absent due to illness or injury on said date, are eligible employees under the Plan. A corporate officer shall be considered employed on a full-time basis if said officer customarily works at least seven months in each year and twenty hours in each week. Any person hereafter becoming an officer of the Corporation, employed on a full-time basis, shall be eligible under this Plan.

3. LIMITATIONS

(a) The Corporation shall reimburse any eligible employee without limitation/no more than $_______________________ (cross out one) in any fiscal year for medical care expenses.

(b) Reimbursement or payment provided under this Plan shall be made by the Corporation only in the event and to the extent that such reimbursement or payment is not provided under any insurance policy(ies), whether owned by the Corporation or the employee, or under any other health and accident or wage continuation plan. In the event that there is such an insurance policy or plan in effect, providing for reimbursement in whole or in part, then to the extent of the coverage under such policy or plan, the Corporation shall be relieved of any and all liability hereunder.

4. SUBMISSION OF PROOF

Any eligible employee applying for reimbursement under this Plan shall submit to the Corporation, at least quarterly, all bills for medical care, including premium notices for accident or health insurance, for verification by the Corporation prior to payment. Failure to comply herewith may, at the discretion of the Corporation, terminate such eligible employee's rights to said reimbursement.

5. DISCONTINUATION

This Plan shall be subject to termination at any time by vote of the board of directors of the Corporation; provided, however, that medical care expenses incurred prior to such termination shall be reimbursed or paid in accordance with the terms of this Plan.

6. DETERMINATION

The president shall determine all questions arising from the administration and interpretation of the Plan except where reimbursement is claimed by the president. In such case, determination shall be made by the board of directors.

S 502 (Rev. 2-92)

MICHIGAN DEPARTMENT OF COMMERCE — CORPORATION AND SECURITIES BUREAU

Date Received			**(FOR BUREAU USE ONLY)**

Name

Address

City   State   ZIP Code

EFFECTIVE DATE:

DOCUMENT WILL BE RETURNED TO NAME AND ADDRESS INDICATED ABOVE

CORPORATION IDENTIFICATION NUMBER

ARTICLES OF INCORPORATION
For use by Domestic Nonprofit Corporations
(Please read information and instructions on last page)

Pursuant to the provisions of Act 162, Public Acts of 1982, the undersigned corporation executes the following Articles:

ARTICLE I

The name of the corporation is:

ARTICLE II

The purpose or purposes for which the corporation is organized are:

ARTICLE III

The corporation is organized upon a ________________________ basis.
(stock or nonstock)

1. If organized on a stock basis, the total number of shares which the corporation has authority to issue is
________________________. If the shares are, or are to be, divided into classes, the designation of each class, the number of shares in each class, and the relative rights, preferences and limitations of the shares of each class are as follows:

ARTICLE III (con't)

2. a. If organized on a nonstock basis, the description and value of its real property assets are: (if none, insert "none")

   b. The description and value of its personal property assets are: (if none, insert "none")

   c. The corporation is to be financed under the following general plan:

   d. The corporation is organized on a _________________________________ basis.
   (membership or directorship)

ARTICLE IV

1. The address of the registered office is:

   _________________________________ , Michigan __________
   (Street Address)   (City)   (ZIP Code)

2. The mailing address of the registered office if different than above:

   _________________________________ , Michigan __________
   (P.O. Box)   (City)   (ZIP Code)

3. The name of the resident agent at the registered office is:

   ____

ARTICLE V

The name(s) and address(es) of the incorporator(s) is (are) as follows:

Name   Residence or Business Address

Use space below for additional Articles or for continuation of previous Articles. Please identify any Article being continued or added. Attach additional pages if needed.

I (We), the incorporator(s) sign my (our) name(s) this __________ day of ________________________ , 19 _____ .

______________________________________   ______________________________________

______________________________________   ______________________________________

______________________________________   ______________________________________

______________________________________   ______________________________________

______________________________________   ______________________________________

Name of person or organization
remitting fees:

____

Preparer's name and business
telephone number:

____

(   ) _______________________________

INFORMATION AND INSTRUCTIONS

1. The articles of incorporation cannot be filed until this form, or a comparable document, is submitted.

2. Submit one original copy of this document. Upon filing, a microfilm copy will be prepared for the records of the Corporation and Securities Bureau. The original copy will be returned to the address appearing in the box on the front as evidence of filing.

   Since this document must be microfilmed, it is important that the filing be legible. Documents with poor black and white contrast, or otherwise illegible, will be rejected.

3. This document is to be used pursuant to the provisions of Act 162, P.A. of 1982, by one or more persons for the purpose of forming a domestic nonprofit corporation.

4. Article II—The purpose for which the corporation is organized must be included. It is not sufficient to state that the corporation may engage in any activity within the purposes for which corporations may be organized under the Act.

5. Article III—The corporation must be organized on a stock or nonstock basis. Complete Article III(1) or III(2) as appropriate, but not both. Real property assets are items such as land and buildings. Personal property assets are items such as cash, equipment, fixtures, etc.

6. Article IV—A post office box may not be designated as the address of the registered office.

7. Article V—The Act requires one or more incorporators. The addresses should include a street number and name (or other designation), city and state.

8. This document is effective on the date approved and filed by the Bureau. A later effective date, no more than 90 days after the date of delivery, may be stated as an additional article.

9. This document must be signed in ink by each incorporator listed in Article V. However, if there are 3 or more incorporators, they may, by resolution adopted at the organizational meeting by a written instrument, designate one of them to sign the articles of incorporation on behalf of all of them. In such event, these articles of incorporation must be accompanied by a copy of the resolution duly certified by the acting secretary at the organizational meeting and a statement must be placed in the articles incorporating that resolution into them.

10. Filing fee & Franchise fee (Make remittance payable to State of Michigan. Include corporation name on check or money order) $20.00

11. Mail form and fee to:
    Michigan Department of Commerce
    Corporation and Securities Bureau
    Corporation Division
    P.O. Box 30054
    6546 Mercantile Way
    Lansing, MI 48909
    Telephone: (517) 334-6302

Incorporation Checklist

Action	Pages where discussed	Completed
1. Select your corporate name (**Read** Naming Your Business and Its Products and Services; **Contact The P. Gaines Co. for trade name and trademark searches**)	**50-52**	
2. Prepare your Articles of Incorporation	**52-60**	
3. File your Articles of Incorporation	**60**	
4. Apply for corporate Employer Identification Number	**71**	
5. Notify creditors (in the case of incorporating a going business)	**61**	
6. Order the Corporate Records Book and Seal	**61-62**	
7. Prepare the Preorganization Subscription Agreement (if applicable)	**62-63**	
8. Prepare the Bylaws	**63-65**	
9. Prepare the Minutes of the First Meeting	**65-68**	
10. Issue shares of stock	**68-71**	
11. File Certificate of Assumed Name (if applicable)	**71**	

Index

A

B

T

CREDIT CARD ORDERS

PHONE TOLLFREE 1-800-578-3853

The Black Beauty Corporate Outfit

By special arrangement with Julius Blumberg, Inc., The P. Gaines Co. will provide a complete corporate kit with the following outstanding features:

1. A three-ring Corporate Record Book with 24K gold trim and lustrous black vinyl slip case. Corporate name is printed on a gold label and inserted into acetate label holder. Record Book includes a Stock Transfer Ledger of 8 pages, bound in a separate section, Mylar-coated Index Tabs, with five important divisions, 50 blank sheets of rag content 20-lb. bond Minute Paper, and exclusive Corporate Record Tickler.

2. A Corporate Seal stored inside the Corporate Record Book in a zipper pouch, 1 5/8" diameter, custom finished with corporate name, state, and year. Long corporate names (over 45 characters and spaces) require a 2" diameter seal, at an extra charge of $7.00.

3. 20 custom printed and numbered Stock Certificates with full page numbered stubs. Each certificate is custom printed with corporate name, state, and officers' titles.

ORDER FORM—Remit with payment to The P. Gaines Co., Box 2253, Oak Park, IL 60303

For all corporate kit orders, please type or print the following information:

Corporate name exactly as on certificate of incorporation...

State of incorporation...

Year of incorporation...

Officers who will sign share certificates (President and Secretary-Treasurer will be listed unless specified otherwise)...

Basic price of corporate kit	<u>$59.95</u>
For long corporate names	
(over 45 characters and spaces), add an additional $7.00	_.__
Shipping by UPS (delivery within 2 weeks from receipt of your order)	<u>4.00</u>
OR Shipping by Air Express (delivery within 4 days from receipt of order)	<u>25.00</u>
(*4-day Air Express orders must be paid for with Certified Check or Money Order)	
TOTAL	_

Ship to:

Your name..Address...
(Street address required)

City..State..Zip.......................

New from P. Gaines

*Five Easy Steps to Setting Up
an IRS-Approved Retirement Plan
for Your Small Business (Incorporated
or Unincorporated), With Forms*

"Less than 20 percent of small businesses in this country have retirement plans for their employees. As a result, businesses with 25 or fewer employees cover an average of only one in seven workers with company pension plans."

With this premise in mind, a new book by Phillip Williams, *Five Easy Steps to Setting Up an IRS-Approved Retirement Plan for Your Small Business*, begins. The key problem is shown to be a lack of money only *sometimes*. Typically, it is either poor planning or a lack of awareness, due to a complete absence of even the most basic information about the subject. *Five Easy Steps. . .* focuses on the message that almost any business that is profitable enough to pay its employee(s) a salary can now start a pension fund under recently passed federal legislation.

Drolly illustrated and wittily written, *Five Easy Steps. . .* takes a fresh look at the familiar conundrum of Chateau d'Yquem taste on a diet cola budget and today's version of the story of the grasshopper and the ant-with-a-pension-plan. The book shows the advantages of Simplified Employee Pensions (SEPs) for most small businesses, whether self-employed (sole proprietors), partnerships, or corporations, and walks the reader step-by-step through the process of setting up and maintaining an SEP. All needed IRS forms are appended.

Five Easy Steps. . . shows why an SEP allows complete funding flexibility, with a retirement arrangement that may be employer financed, employee financed, or a combination of each. It points out that the percentage of employee salaries to be contributed to a retirement plan may be reset *each* year, up to a maximum of 15 percent of salary per employee per year or $30,000, whichever is less. It fully explains the procedure for integrating an SEP with Social Security. It emphasizes other advantages as well, such as the option (not permitted in certain other types of plans) of making contributions in profitable years or skipping pension set-asides entirely in lean years.

Certain disadvantages of SEPs, which might make Keoghs, 401(k) plans, or defined benefit pension plans more attractive under some circumstances are also covered.

This lively and enlightening guide will do more to awaken the American small business person to the necessity of retirement planning and the concrete way to go about it than twenty dry-as-dust books on the same topic from major trade publishers.

> "The first in a series dubbed the Small Business Bookshelf discusses the benefits and variety of IRS-approved retirement programs available to small businesses. . . . A good how-to manual"--American Library Association's *Booklist.*

ISBN 0-936284-33-1

quality paperback, 8 1/2 x 11, $14.95, indexed

CREDIT CARD ORDERS

PHONE TOLLFREE 1-800-578-3853

nall Business Bookshelf Series
olume 2 (ISBN 0-936284-10-2) $19.95

NAMING YOUR BUSINESS AND ITS PRODUCTS AND SERVICES:
How To Create Effective Trade Names, Trademarks, and Service Marks To Attract Customers, Protect Your Good Will And Reputation, And Stay Out Of Court

/ery business, no matter how small, needs a company trade name. In addition, manufacturers and com-
nies providing services to the public may require distinctive names for their goods (trademarks) and ser-
ces (service marks). This book explains the crucial differences between these three types of names used in
mmerce, the name selection process, and the legal cautions and pitfalls.

»pics covered include:
- The difference between trademarks, copyrights, and patents
- What determines ownership of a trademark or service mark
- Why trade names are *not* registrable with the Patent and Trademark Office (PTO)
- Why *all* trade names, whether used by sole proprietors, partnerships, or corporations, should be "cleared" r possible infringements of other trade names, trademarks, and service marks
- Why existing businesses that failed to research their trade names for possible legal violations before going to business should do so *now*, instead of later
- Why clearance of a name by the Corporation Division of a given state offers no guarantee of trademark or ade name clearance
- How to do computer and manual trademark and trade name searches, including the use of the RADEMARKSCAN® data base, Shepard's *Citations,* and industry and trade directories
- Iow what you don't know *can* hurt you in the realm of trademark law
- The main differences between state and federal trademark laws
- The 8 advantages of federal trademark registration
- The federal trademark registration process; the differences between the Principal Register and the Secon- ry Register
- Why family surnames are disallowed as registrable trademarks or service marks by the PTO, with one ex- ption
- The risks and rewards of names that parody or satirize, such as LARDASHE® jeans for overweight people
- Why you do *not* have to register your trademark or service mark with the PTO in order to use the symbol™
- Why you *must* register your trademark or service mark with the PTO to use the symbol ®
- Why a term that is "merely descriptive" of a company's goods or services, such as "Lite" (for a type of beer) "Super glue"(for a type of super-adhesive) cannot be registered as a trademark
- The use of symbols, puns, and historical, mythical, and literary allusions as effective marks
- Name-coining techniques

The P. Gaines Co. now offers computer trademark and service mark searches and company name searches. **Both types of seach include:** (1) a computer search of Dun and Bradstreet's Electronic Business Directory, a listing of some 9 million U.S. businesses; (2) a computer search of TRADEMARKSCAN®, scanning both the currently active state and federal trademark registra- tions in all classes; (3) a computer search of TRADE NAME DATABASE, consisting of trade names and common law trademarks (not registered) as well as registered trademarks compiled by Gale Research in Brands and Their Companies.; (4) a search of some 20 additional data bases where business names appear is also included. Check the order form for additional information.

HOW TO FORM YOUR OWN CORPORATION BEFORE THE *INC.* DRIES!

Illinois Incorporation, 3rd ed. (ISBN 0-936284-29-3)	**$24.95**
Ohio Incorporation, 1st ed. (ISBN 0-936284-39-0)	**$19.95**
Michigan Incorporation, 2st ed. (ISBN 0-936284-06-4)	**$24.95**
Indiana Incorporation, 1st ed. (ISBN 0-936284-18-8)	**$19.95**
Missouri Incorporation, 1st ed. (ISBN 0-936284-02-1)	**$19.95**

The world's most perfect tax shelter is no longer the private preserve of the rich and the savvy. Even one-person businesses, whether that of the consultant, the artist, or the professional practitioner, can now incorporate and enjoy many of the same benefits as the largest multinational corporations. Each of the volumes in the Small Business Incorporation Series fully explains the advantages, as well as the disadvantages, of incorporation and shows how almost anyone, from the successful hobbyist to the small business owner, can incorporate today at surprisingly low cost and enjoy numerous tax write-offs, limit personal liability, achieve greater financial flexibility, and obtain additional retirement and other benefits not otherwise available to partnerships and the self-employed (sole proprietors).

While there exist general books on incorporation, each of the manuals in the series walks the reader step by step through the incorporation process of a *specific* state and provides all needed state-mandated forms in a tear-out format, including Articles of Incorporation, Bylaws, Minutes, and even Stock Certificates. Each guide covers regular for-profit corporations in depth, as well as professional service corporations, S corporations, not-for-profit corporations, and Delaware and Nevada corporations. Other features include a surprisingly detailed index and a comprehensive incorporation checklist giving the steps required to incorporate, in their proper sequence, the pages numbers of the book where each activity is discussed, and a column to indicate the completion of each step.

Book Order Form

Remit check or M.O. with order to The P. Gaines Co., PO Box 2253, Oak Park, IL 60303

Credit Card Orders: Mail in order (supply information below) or call tollfree: 1-800-578-3853

Title	No. of copies	Price per copy	Total
Five Steps to Setting Up a Retirement Plan	_______	$14.95	_______
Illinois Incorporation Manual (3rd ed)	_______	$24.95	_______
Michigan Incorporation Manual (2nd ed)	_______	$24.95	_______
Ohio Incorporation Manual (1st ed)	_______	$19.95	_______
Indiana Incorporation Manual (1st ed)	_______	$19.95	_______
Missouri Incorporation Manual (1st ed)	_______	$19.95	_______
Naming Your Business (Trademarks)	_______	$19.95	_______
Subtotal			_______
7.75% sales tax (Illinois residents only)			_______
Shipping ($2.00 for first book; $1.00 for each additional title)			_______
TOTAL			

Name..Address...Phone.........................

Charge to my: ______Visa ______Mastercard Card #:___________________________________Expires:__________